YOU CAN TAKE THE BOY OUT OF THE BAY

The Memoirs of Thomas Graham Morry of Ferryland

Thomas Graham Morry

Edited by

Christopher J. A. Morry

Cover Photo

The cover photo shows three Morry brothers, Bill, Tom and Reg, in Ferryland, ca. 1928. It can be taken for granted from the outfits that they are wearing that this was a Sunday, probably after attending Mass. The photo was taken by their aunt, Trix Giovannetti, a skillful amateur photographer.

YOU CAN TAKE THE BOY OUT OF THE BAY*

The Memoirs of Thomas Graham Morry of Ferryland

Thomas Graham Morry

Edited by

Christopher J. A. Morry

* An old Newfoundland expression: *"You can take the boy out of the bay, but you can't take the bay out of the boy"*. Particularly apt in the case of Thomas Graham Morry.

Avalonia & Hibernia Enterprises
4-160D Edwards St.
Rockland, Ontario K4K 1H9
www.avalonia-hibernia.ca

Copyright © 2019 Christopher J. A. Morry
Library and Archives Canada Cataloguing in Publication
Morry, Christopher, 1949-, editor

You Can Take the Boy Out of the Bay: The Memoirs of Thomas Graham Morry of Ferryland / Author – Thomas Graham Morry; Edited by Christopher J. A. Morry.
ISBN 978-1-7753535-2-2 (Bound)
ISBN 978-1-7753535-3-9 (eBook)

1. Thomas Graham Morry, 1919-2008 - Biography. 2. Newfoundland, 1920 – 1950. Personal Narratives. 3. Ferryland, Newfoundland – Personal Narratives. 4. Eastern United States, 1935 - 1940 – Personal Narratives. 5. Newfoundland Confederation -- History

Previous page: Ferryland Northside, ca 1950, showing the Barnable, Johnston, Morry and Deveraux fishing stages (nearest to farthest). This photograph was used on a popular postcard sold for many years by Tooton's Photography located on Water St. in St. John's. This copy was amongst the papers of T. G. Morry.

All Rights Reserved. No part of this publication may be reproduced, stored in a retrieval system or transmitted, in any form or by any means, without the prior written consent of the publishers or a license from The Canadian Copyright Licensing Agency (Access Copyright). For an Access Copyright license, visit www.accesscopyright.ca or call toll-free to 1-800-893-5777.

For Dad and his brothers and sisters…

Not because they were all that different from the others with whom they grew up, but precisely because they were much of a kind – a generation now gone, unique in almost every respect compared to the generations before and since

Christopher J. A. Morry, Editor, April 2019

Contents

Contents vi
Introduction viii
Foreword xii
Chapter 1: School Days 1
Chapter 2: The Church 11
Chapter 3: Childhood Memories 27
Chapter 4: Characters 54
Chapter 5: The "Boston States" in the Dirty Thirties 80
Chapter 6: The War Years and Confederation 88
Chapter 7: Becoming a "CFA" 124
Epilogue/Conclusion 132
Acknowledgments 134
Appendix 135
About the Editor 144

Introduction

As an editor of the work of another, especially, as in this case, a much loved and respected father, there is a natural tendency to want to portray that person in the best possible light and to not bring any negative or pejorative comment to the work one is preparing on his behalf. And, especially in these times, in which we are progressively becoming more and more aware of the concerns and sensitivities of other members of our multicultural and multivariate society, there is a natural tendency to want to tone down, not to say whitewash, expressions and terms no longer considered appropriate, though they may have been entirely acceptable a few decades ago.

Case in point, the constant use of the term "Newfie" in my father's Foreword which follows. I know how offensive the mere use of this term is to many Newfoundlanders. But I am cognizant too of what a proud Newfoundlander my father was, and I am confident that he used this term in the most loving and heartfelt manner. He considered himself to be a "Newf" or a "Newfie" to his dying day and saw no harm in using these words as terms of endearment for his fellow Newfoundlanders. I am therefore reluctant to change his use of this term. That said, and despite his protestations to the contrary in his Preface, Dad did not take the telling of *"Newfy Jokes"* by foreigners (i.e. non-Newfoundlanders) lying down. I know for a fact that he had a whole arsenal of jokes he told with delight on such occasions which ended with the Newfoundlander getting the upper hand on the intolerant Mainlander.

In other respects, I think that the average Newfoundland reader will find much to commend itself in the stories which I have included in this brief anthology. There were many others, but these, I think, capture the essence of growing up in outport Newfoundland during the Depression, as well as in the US in the

Dirty Thirties, St. John's during and after WWII, and also before and after Confederation. There is a brief final chapter which touches on my father's first experiences as a Newfoundlander and a Public Servant in Ottawa in the 1950s and 60s.

My father inherited a knack for storytelling from his father, Howard, a well-known raconteur in Ferryland and the surrounding area. Also, his uncle, John, was a past master at this form of entertainment and, if anything, had a better grasp of how to stretch the truth without completely breaking it. The problem was and is that you never knew whether a story they told was true, partly true, or a total fabrication. For the most part, I suspect that these stories were passed around and embellished as they were told and retold, and finally were adopted by my father as "his", though he may never have been present when the events being recounted took place if indeed they ever occurred. I had even thought of entitling this book *"Lies My Father Told Me"*, only I suspect that the author of the short story of that name and the director of that now famous Canadian movie based on the short story would have taken umbrage.

A few words on my father's upbringing may be useful to put in context what you read. Dad was the third child in a family that would eventually see nine children born, though one died in early childhood. This was fairly typical of the size of families in Newfoundland at the time, especially in the outports. He was born in 1919, in one of those outports, Ferryland, on the Southern Shore. As he observes in his Foreword, the community into which he was born was an amalgam of English and Irish cultures, with the Scottish culture of his war-bride mother superimposed, in his family, as it was in a few others in the surrounding area. The only real difference between his family and most of the others in the village was that, in the beginning, when the Morrys first came to Newfoundland, they were English merchants, while most of their neighbours were Irish fishermen-farmers. The distinction was probably an important one in the late 18th and early 19th centuries but had become decidedly less important by the early 20th century, after economic losses, particularly the bank collapse of 1894, destroyed the fortunes of many merchant families, including the Morrys. From that point forward, they made their living by hands-on work in the fishery like everyone else but were fortunate enough to be able to subsidize that meagre income as post-masters and the owners of small shops. But really, the only important distinction in the family in my estimation was the outside influence of Dad's mother, who had been born and raised in Edinburgh, and who had different experiences than others in the village – experiences that naturally coloured her children's world view.

Thomas Graham Morry at 76
Photo by Yousuf Karsh

Foreword

Editor's Notes:

What follows is an introduction to my father's written memoirs in his own words. I have not altered this section, as it provides a better context to the anecdotes that follow than I could possibly write.

Dad's memoirs came to me as a legacy of sorts. I was his Executor and, amongst his papers, I discovered a simple brown manila file folder with these words on the cover:

"Chris: you may be interested; destroy if not of some use. Dad. Personal notes of days long gone by. Mar. 4/07"

Inside the folder were 137 pages written out in his inimitable and frequently illegible handwriting. Luckily for me, he had the foresight to record on six mini audio tapes all of the anecdotes he had written down. Despite the poor sound quality, with these as a backup, I was able to transcribe and record the stories contained in this book, which are only a selection of those he originally penned.

As I stare at the blank page before me, which is destined to be the first page of a book which I have been thinking of for some time, I find myself unable to determine an original introductory approach. What follows is essentially a collection of recollections and anecdotes concerning my childhood in that cradle of independence and individuality, the "outports" of Newfoundland.

In these days it is the *"in"* thing to have a ready supply of *"Newfie"* jokes to regale the gathering at coffee break or during the cocktail hour. It is the Newfie's turn now that the Irish, German, Polish, Hungarian, Greek, French Canadians and others have in their turn been the butt of such jokes. Whether this has a psychological aspect I will not conjecture. I will be satisfied in saying that the stories, although they wound many Newfies are frequently told with affection and rarely with rancour.

Where the Newfie being somewhat insular, as are by simple definition all other islanders, often resents comments made by "outsiders", he spends a good deal of time poking fun at himself and his fellow islanders.

A typical example of this is the statement of Newfies that John Cabot, who discovered Newfoundland, got £10 for doing so but he should have gotten 10 years instead! I've heard Newfies say this or something like it in one breath and in the next respond vehemently to a mild statement by an outsider about the weather (a sensitive subject raised by only the bravest or most foolish "Mainlander" in conversation with a Newfoundlander).

There is always evident in Newfies a fierce pride and sense of independence, born of almost 500 years of tenacious existence in spite of some of the worst adversities ever faced by man. Nothing comes easy in the rugged land and nothing easy is expected.

As I pause at this point and reflect, I know now that the motivation to write this book was not a desire to earn money. The audience to whom it will appeal is bound to be small. It will consist mainly of Newfies, ex-Newfies (I'm sure there is no such person – once a Newfie always a Newfie), those who know and admire them, and possibly a few casual readers who will buy the book because they've heard about the crazy Newfies. One thing is certain, that while much of my adult life has been spent outside the island, I am not an unbiased observer and my affection for the place of my birth and its people is bound to colour my recollections.

Very little continuity is involved in this book. I am merely telling anecdotes as I recall them and providing some coherent pattern in their presentation. I will not knowingly embellish or change what are essentially representational stories which reflect the character of the Newfie and particularly those of the outports.
The population of the island is almost completely drawn from English, Irish and Scottish stock and there has been a

considerable blending of the bloodstreams, accents and cultures of these groups.

This has resulted in a unique individual who possesses the attributes of all three, although many of these attributes are in constant conflict.

In the area where I was born and where I spent a happy childhood in spite of what would probably be classed today as poverty or near poverty, the blend I spoke of above has resulted, in many cases, in people who have the English gift of understatement, the tenacious characteristics of the Scot and the wit and mercurial temperament of the Irish. These ingredients in themselves are the seed of a very interesting crop. Added to this is the history of deprivation and hardship and the hazardous occupation of fishermen which exacted its toll in lives and hardship but created a philosophical approach to adversity.

So now let us pursue some anecdotes which are truly representational in that they portray the characteristics of the breed which have evolved from the genetic and environmental conditions referred to earlier.

Tom Morry Overlooking Scenes from his Youth ca 1943
Morry Family Collection

Chapter 1: School Days

*Howard Morry with his first three children, Phyllis, Bill and Tom, ca 1921
Morry Family Collection*

Editor's Notes:

Dad's reflections on his earliest years attending primary and secondary school at the parochial school associated with Holy Trinity Parish in Ferryland are a slice in time. Those of us in later generations love to make fun of our elders for telling us of the hardships that they had to endure when they were young. Well, how many of us had to bring junks of wood or lumps of coal to school in the morning, or jockey for a place close to the pot belly stove in order to keep warm while trying to concentrate on what was being taught? These were indeed conditions that even people in my generation can hardly credit, and my grandchildren's schools would be shut down if they failed to provide such basic necessities in this manner.

Perhaps that is precisely why he, and most likely his fellow classmates, looked back at those times and focussed on the amusing things that occasionally lightened their days.

In the stories in this chapter and those that follow in subsequent chapters, I have hidden the identity of the people mentioned. Dad wrote the stories that way, but forgot when he was making the audio tapes, and used their real names. I could have substituted the real names in his written accounts for the book. Where I have substituted pseudonyms, it is more to give the stories a more universal appeal rather than to serve as a form of censorship. In instances where the stories might have proved somewhat embarrassing, it was easier to simply leave them out of the anthology, as there was ample material of all sorts to choose from. Many of these stories would have made the rounds in the village being told over and over again and therefore have likely been preserved in the minds of some children and grandchildren, as indeed they were more than "twice-told tales" to me and my siblings. On a few occasions, I have used the real name of a person because that person was so well-known and well-loved that it would make little sense to attempt to hide their identity.

What does not come up in Dad's retelling of his time in school is that there was only one school in Ferryland in those days, and it was an all-Catholic school. Those familiar with other outports around the coast of Newfoundland, where there were frequently two or three religions present, and two or three schools to educate their respective children, will find this strange. Indeed, it is a fact that Ferryland too once had a substantial English Anglican population (including the Morry family in those days, before they converted) with their own church, presbytery, parish hall and school. These were located just to the north of the Catholic convent, school, church and hall mentioned here.

But, with the passage of time, the Roman Catholics began to outnumber the Anglicans, and institutions supporting the Anglican faith fell, one by one. It would have been during the time represented by the events in this chapter that St. Luke's Anglican Church finally fell into such disrepair that it had to be deconsecrated and taken down. Those few remaining members of the Anglican faith in Ferryland would have had to travel the two or three miles (three to five kilometres) to Aquaforte to attend St. Philip the Apostle Church. As for schooling, most Anglicans who could afford it reluctantly sent their children away to St. John's to be educated. Some not so well-to-do may have had to send their children to the Catholic school.

Many writers have dealt with this subject, and some renowned books and plays have been devoted to the bitter-sweet memories of school days. It has always seemed to me a great pity that few, if any of us, appreciates school until we are adults, at which stage nostalgia clouds the vision.

Sadly, the only photo in existence of the Morry Family at this time, ca 1931 Back from left to right: Howard (father) Phyllis, Bill, Fredris (mother, with Priscilla in her arms); middle row, Reg, Bill and Tom; front row, Jean, Kay and Elsie.
Morry Family Collection

I have to say that, on the whole, I enjoyed going to school. I was blessed with a retentive memory and didn't have to work hard, and also, from birth, my parents had concentrated on indoctrinating all eight of us with the desirability of getting a good education for its own sake and to ensure escape from the hard life of the fisherman. School seemed to be a small price to pay, and besides, it was rather pleasant to spend time in play, because when school was out there was always work to be done in the fishery, on the farm or about the property.

At the time I started school, it was customary for the boys of the village to go to school only until they were big enough to go fishing with their fathers, although some of them would continue school for a few months during the winter months. It was scarcely considered manly to continue school on a regular basis until high school graduation, and there had been very few male high school graduates from the school until my generation. Even though times had changed and were continuing to change when I finished my high school education, I was the only boy in a graduating class of ten.

Howard Morry and two of the children haying
Morry Family Collection

My first day in school was May 24, 1924, when I was about 4 ½ years old. I do not know why I started on that day. It was Victoria Day and I got a chance to hold the flag with the assistance of one of the Sisters who taught in the school.

The school was run by the Presentation Sisters and all teachers were nuns. They were, in the main, a well-educated, well-motivated, sensitive group and I often wonder at the sense of dedication which enabled them to survive and thrive in the environment of an outport school. The children were polite and courteous it's true, but many of them had a streak of individuality and devilment which would tax the patience and ingenuity of a psychologist.

The school was a one-storey structure built of masonry, which reclined on the side of a hill. It was situated between the convent and the Church and was connected to both by a covered passageway. The school had two classrooms, each of which was heated by a large, round wood or coal stove.

There was never, to my memory, enough coal to keep the schoolrooms heated during the winter, and sometimes there was no coal at all. In such circumstances, each child was required to bring a piece of wood, referred to locally as a "junk", to keep the fire going during the day. The fire was allowed to die during the night and each morning had to be lit just before the beginning of first classes. Usually, a boy in each classroom was delegated on a weekly basis to start the fire and ensure that it burned during the day.

Convent, School, Church and Church Hall, Ferryland, ca 1930
Courtesy Ida [White] Michael

Generally, the fire burned well, but there was never enough heat to keep the rooms at a liveable temperature. Thus, on very cold, windy days, it was sometimes necessary to send the children home. An added hazard was that, when the wind blew in a certain direction, there was a down-draft from the hill which drove the smoke from the chimney back into the schoolroom.

It was not long before we discovered an easy way to get out early, particularly when the ice was in condition for hockey or there was good snow for sliding. The usual procedure was for a limited few boys (those in the know) to decide it was time for a half holiday.

At noon, while the Sisters were at table, and the other students were gone home to eat, the delegated two boys would climb the roof from the side of the hill and place a small piece of heavy iron or a flat rock on the chimney, making sure not to cover the top completely, but also ensuring that enough smoke would stay inside to cause early closing. The explanation to the Sisters was always the same: *"the wind is coming down from the hill."* In all the time at school, and in spite of many occasions when the weather was very nice and the *"wind came down from the hill"*, the Sisters never suspected the real reason for the smoke.

Poverty was a continuing companion of the majority of students in the school. They were, for the most part, ill-fed and ill-housed, especially during the Depression. The unfortunate result was not only early drop-outs and absenteeism and poor scholarship, but a plague of tuberculosis (TB) which sometimes decimated whole families. I do not know how many students died of TB in their teens, but the numbers were surely disproportionate in comparison with any other western country.

In spite of lack of worldly goods, most children attended school at some time during the year and, during the fall, the slack season for the fishery, and post-harvest, the majority were in attendance. Each of the school's two rooms had two or three teachers, depending on the number of classes. Each teacher taught a number of classes, usually three.

At the time, the teachers were, as I have said earlier, Sisters of the Presentation order, a well-educated, hard-working group. It is easy to understand that religion formed a major part of the curriculum. Each day began with a prayer and at 12 o'clock there was a half hour of religious instruction. The total room took part in this half hour, during which we were told of the importance of religion, the importance of telling the truth, the need to say prayers the first thing in the morning and the last at night.

The instructing Sister was always sure to ask one or more of the students by name to stand and say what was the first thing they did when they awoke in the morning. Usually, the reply was "I said my prayers", regardless of whether this was true or not, as it avoided a lot of argument and perhaps some form of penance if the response was not suitable.

One day, after a particularly strong instruction period on the importance of truth and the likelihood of losing one's immortal soul and going to hell if a lie was told, the teacher remembered just before dismissing the class for lunch that she had not asked the usual question. The teacher called out to one boy selected at random *"Quickly now, what did you do first thing this morning as soon as you got up"*? The boy rose and, despite his being embarrassed to admit it, but probably remembering the dire consequences of lying, decided to tell the truth. He said loudly and clearly, *"I pissed."*

To say that there was pandemonium in the room for several minutes is an understatement. Imagine 60 children trying to keep from laughing and not succeeding. Fortunately, the Sister, who was either shocked or possibly as amused as we were (nuns in outports, in particular, had to get used to some pretty straight language), pulled her veil across her face and hurriedly left the classroom and never mentioned the incident afterwards.

We were always reminded by the teachers to close the school door when we entered and left to prevent the sheep and goats, who roamed at will, feeding on the grass near the school, from entering. But sometimes we would forget and, if a storm were brewing, the animals would decide to shelter in the school, creating havoc and merriment, if it was during school hours, and another kind of havoc as you can imagine if they entered and spent the night with nowhere else to leave the results of their digestion.

On one occasion, they entered after school and, while they were later driven out, a few who hid passed the night inside with predictable results. In the morning, the early students tried to put things to order but they were guilty of one oversight, as was revealed later.

Each morning, we knelt and prayed for five or ten minutes to start the day right, and woe betide anyone who broke the meditation and cadence of prayer, regardless of the reason. This particular morning, we had just commenced prayers when a small child arose and approached the Sister calling *"Sister Mary, look what I found on the floor"*. The Sister opened her eyes and placed her finger on her lips, but the child would not be deterred and, perhaps not understanding the signal, continued to approach and said more loudly *"Sister, look what I found on the floor"*.

At this point, the Sister, recognizing the inevitability of interruption, and recognizing the child was too young to realize the gravitas of his crime, asked the child to come forward and tell her what he had found. He approached, opened his hand and, placed it as near as possible to the Sister's face to reveal the contents, which I think that you can imagine!

By this time all of the students were consumed with laughter and prayers came to an abrupt end. The sight of the teacher trying to remain calm and solemn only added to the merriment until she was forced to flee to recover her composure. I'll never forget the incident and I'm sure every student present will never forget.
One of the exercises prescribed in the school for the more senior students was to read aloud some poetry and then explain its

meaning. One day, the Sister called on one of the shyest pupils in the school, to read a part of an epic poem which begins with the words *"Cease now thy rage and lay thine ire aside..."*. He started *"Case now thy rage..."*, never having seen the word "cease" written before. At which point the teacher interrupted and said *"Cease!"*. He did as he was told, and sat down with relief. She then ordered him to rise and recommence, ending with the same result. By this time, the teacher, who evidently had a very limited sense of humour, and who thought that she was being made the butt of a joke, was quite angry and, after the usual corporal punishment, ordered the boy to write the offending passage 100 times.

He was obviously flustered and frightened, for next day he handed in his lines: *"Case now thy rage..."* written 100 times. By then the teacher recognized there was a block and explained the difference to him. I would think he never forgot how to spell "cease" correctly after that experience!

My younger brother, Reg, was my best friend in our youth. There were only two years separating us in age. He and I were more of a handful for our parents. Our older brother, Bill, was ill and bedridden for over a year with rheumatic fever, possibly triggered by a bout of scarlet fever in his early years. This seems to have taken a lot of the rebelliousness out of him – at least when we were growing up.

What we did not know, and did not learn until decades later, was that Reg was ill too, in his case with an illness only diagnosed much later as narcolepsy. Narcolepsy is a form of neural disease that manifests itself in various types of sleep disorders. Later in life, when it was getting much worse, Reg would be talking with you and, if he got the least bit excited about what he was saying, he would slump down to the floor in a sort of faint, more than a seizure. It would take him about five minutes to recover on his own and, after that, it was as if nothing had happened.

But when we were young the symptom most notable to others was that when Reg went to sleep the doomsday gun would not awaken him. And when the rest of us woke up at the normal time to have breakfast and get ready for school, many times there was no way to awaken Reg. You could shake him all you liked and he would just slumber on.

One time when this happened it was a Monday morning. The night before Reg flaked out with all his clothes on, including his Sunday best shirt and tie. I tried my darndest to wake him and get him to come down and have his breakfast, but nothing was getting through to him. As the time came to leave for school with the school bell expected within 10 minutes (we lived about a km from the school), I gave it one last unsuccessful try and then had to give up or I would be late too.

About an hour later, Reg came out of it, more or less, realised he was late for school, jumped out of bed, got dressed and beat it up the main road to school reaching it in record time. He rushed through the door and went to find his seat and wondered why everyone was laughing. It turned out that he had forgotten that he was already dressed and had hastily pulled another pair of pants and another shirt and even another tie over the clothes he had on already in his haste before leaving the house.

Reg was a happy go lucky, friendly lad and was always a favourite in the village, then just as he was many years later when he came back from the war to run the fish business for our father. So needless to say, after a quick snicker or two, all his schoolmates felt really sorry for him, as did the Sister, and not a word was spoken when he went out behind the school to take off the extra set of clothes and then came back into the classroom and sat at his desk.

Chapter 2: The Church

Holy Trinity RC Church, Ferryland
(Ten Historic Towns: Heritage Architecture in Newfoundland; Valhalla Press, by arrangement with the Newfoundland Historic Trust; St. John's (N.L.); 1978)

Editor's Notes:

Without getting into too much of a history lesson, Ferryland's earliest roots go back to its settlement by George Calvert (later Lord Baltimore) in 1621.

One particularly interesting fact about this settlement, which only lasted less than a decade, is that it was founded in a spirit of religious tolerance. It is said that Calvert was himself a Catholic, though it did not do to be too open about it then. One of the prime motivations for his seeking to establish a settlement in the New World (he later had greater success in founding Maryland) was to provide a safe haven not only for Catholics but for people of all faiths.

Though the Colony of Avalon was a failure, it seems that this spirit of ecumenism prevailed unofficially thereafter in the successful settlement that followed.

What government there was in Newfoundland in the 17th and 18th centuries was no more broad-minded in terms of religious tolerance than the government at home in England, since they took their marching orders from London. But that said, the people themselves got on tolerably well together regardless of faith. Indeed, the only discussion of religious riots in Ferryland in those days was between factions of Irish disagreeing over who their priest should be. English Protestants and Irish Roman Catholics more or less learned to live and let live, though indeed, when women finally began to arrive in Newfoundland, there were precious few mixed marriages.

This situation more or less prevailed through the 19th and into the 20th century, possibly even improving over the years because of the increasing number of mixed marriages that began to occur in this period. Such was the case with the Morry family in the time of Dad's grandparents. His grandfather, also Thomas Graham Morry, was as staunch an Anglican man as they came: didn't drink, smoke or swear, prayed daily and never lost his temper. He married Kate White, of Irish Roman Catholic stock and, as they say, they quite literally lived and loved happily ever after.

So, the Morrys became Catholics, leaving only the Carters and a very few other smaller families to keep the faith with the Anglican church until their numbers in Ferryland dwindled in the early to mid-1900s when, as mentioned above, the Anglican parish church, which was over one hundred years old at the time, finally closed its doors.

Ironically, in the next generation, it was a complete reversal of what happened with Thomas and Kate. Howard Morry, Dad's father, was raised a Roman Catholic, as noted above. He went overseas in WWI with the Royal Newfoundland Regiment and there fell in love with a Scottish lass named Fredris Minty. Fredris' family was staunch United Free Church of Scotland, a small breakaway group from the official Church of Scotland whose views were more humanist than religious and whose strongest belief was in the biblical admonition to provide charity cheerfully to those in need. Yet when Fredris came to Ferryland she adapted (though she did not convert) and always attended Mass with the family and even played the organ in the church and sang in the choir. I've been told, and I believe it to be true, that she was one of the most beloved women in the village
because of her universal kindness and generosity, regardless of her religious beliefs.

Note that in this chapter I am leaving in the name of the priest, Father Sheehan, who was well-loved and respected in the village and who, if he were alive today, would not object, as he could take a little gentle ribbing like this in stride.

The Roman Catholic Church which I referred to earlier is one of the oldest stone structures in North America *[Editor's Note: Dad has his facts wrong here; the church was only built starting in 1863 and continuing to 1898]* and the centre of all activities in the village during my youth. The Priest was a leader of the community in

more ways than one and was expected to be the advisor and counsellor in all matters, whether family finances, illnesses, love, marriage, or family quarrels were involved, as well as ministering to the spiritual needs of the congregation of course.

During the Great Depression, the Priest, as well as the villagers, lived a hand-to-mouth existence. There was a system which required that each head of family contributed to the Priest's upkeep on an annual basis, but often when money was scarce these annual "dues" were paid in kind: fish, fowl, beef, wood, or anything which was produced by the villagers. There was also one day when each fisherman donated his total catch to the Church.

The weekly collection during Mass was designed to take care of the day to day minor needs of the Church, but it never did, to my knowledge. The actual collection contained 50¢ or 20¢ from the merchant, the same from the doctor, a sprinkling of dimes and nickels, a large collection of 1¢ pieces, an occasional medal, and any other coin-like object available that would make it sound like the donor was actually putting a coin into the collection plate.

The altar boys usually took the collection and I recall one Sunday as I proceeded with the collection box, I was asked did I take eggs. During that period eggs were bartered at the two village stores for necessities such as yeast cake, salt, pepper, etc. and presumably my questioner was giving the impression that he was prepared to contribute to the Sunday collection in the same fashion.

In addition to the usual annual or monthly dues, other sources of income were used, including concerts, garden parties, picture shows, etc., but usually the Priest was able to live in reasonable comfort only if he had good friends who contributed to his upkeep.

The Priest understood how difficult the times were and never complained when a truly destitute family failed to meet its obligations. But there were some parishioners, who were the most visible delinquents, who could well afford to pay but did not, and whose concerns absorbed a greater share of the Priests efforts than others in the parish. In such cases, it was not unusual for the Priest to ask for his dues if he met such a non-payer in the street, and it did not usually make any difference if other persons were present. It was also not unusual for the Priest to tackle a non-payer in the confessional, preferably after the confession of sins but before the giving of absolution. I doubt that absolution was ever denied for this reason, but many promises to pay were no doubt a result of such tactics.

Another form of persuasion was to post a list on the door of the Church where it would be seen by all of the flock. The list would contain the list of the names of all employed persons and the amount of their donations.

This too was an effective expedient which would often be buttressed by an announcement of names and donations from the pulpit.

There were, however, always some holdouts who perhaps became more determined than ever not to pay each time a new tactic was introduced. I'll give you an example. On Sunday morning when one particular delinquent arrived at Church, he saw the customary list on the door. He paused to scrutinise it carefully. Although he was not interested in paying, he was interested in who had paid and how much they had paid.

As he scanned the list, his eye was suddenly caught by his name and, on closer examination, he saw the notation *"never paid"*. He immediately decided to bring the record up to date and went to the house next door to the Church to borrow a pen or pencil. He then returned to the Church door, after which he laboriously added a further note opposite his name – *"no and never will"*. This action caused much merriment in the village and had the effect of hardening the attitude of some other backsliders. The result was predictable. The list was removed and the Priest reverted to other tried and true remedies, but that was the last time such a list was ever posted in the village.

Interior of Holy Trinity as it appears today and most likely back then
Photo by the editor, 2018

Despite their general poverty, however, the residents held onto their sense of humour and independence. They became masters at using everything that could be used for clothing. For example, old tyres were used to mend shoes and flour sacks were used to make shirts, dresses and sometimes underclothes. Many people bleached the flour sacks to remove the brand before using them to make clothing, but sometimes, if the need was great, the clothes were made and worn and bleached subsequently. This practice was not only followed for children, but adults too sometimes used flour sacks to make clothing. This no doubt led to increased modesty lest anyone see *"Purity Flour"* emblazoned on their undergarments!

The Church had a high domed roof which had to be tarred once each year and one of the village handymen usually did the job. To get to the top it was necessary to use a long ladder to get to the eave and another ladder for the dome. These ladders were hoisted on ropes which were tied to the iron railing near the building. One day, when the roof was being prepared, my brother and I lowered the ladder, marooning the carpenter on the roof. When he hollered at us and told us what he would do when he got down, we panicked and ran, leaving him sitting astride the roof using language which the Church does not normally hear. It was more than an hour before some passerby heard his cries and came to his rescue, but for a long time afterwards, whenever we saw him, we disappeared as rapidly as possible.

[Editor's Note: Just for the record and to protect the innocent, the brother mentioned would be his younger brother, Reg. Tom and Reg were co-conspirators in many adventures and much devilment; their eldest brother, Bill, was a serious lad and would never consider being involved in such tricks. Well, so I'm told!]

During the years 7 to 15, most boys served as altar boys, or occasionally both altar boys and members of the choir. I recall one occasion when a number of us were delegated to join the regular members of the choir on a day when there was a special service. We were to join in the singing of some well-known hymns. The choir loft was situated in the back of the Church and many members of the congregation sat below, and the space immediately underneath was used as standing room, when the attendance made this necessary.

We commenced by having target practice with spit-balls on the bald heads below, and many a perplexed man felt liquid on his head without any rational explanation. It was not for this alone, however, for our game became known to the choir-master, but the lusty rendering of some of the hymns with words of our own personal contribution, such as *"I'm not going to work anymore, I'll live on the fat of me guts"*, which replaced a very soulful and solemn passage which ended *"I'll live on the flesh of my God"*. I can still remember the shock on the face of the Sister, who was also the choir-master. I can assure you that our service as members of the choir was probably the briefest on record.

The Mass in those days was said in Latin and us altar boys (there was no such thing as an altar girl at the time) learned by rote all the responses we were expected to make to the priest's words, and many of us also wound up knowing the priest's words as well. I never forgot those and could probably say a Latin Mass from beginning to end today if asked to do so.

Of course, boys being boys, we liked to play around a little with the words and hope that the priest did not catch on. One response, spoken correctly was: *"Ad Deum qui laetificat, juventutem meam"*, which I found out later means: *"To God, who brings joy to my youth"*, though of course, we hadn't a clue what it meant at the time. In any event, we preferred our own version which went: *"Ad Deum qui three legs on a cat juventutem mean."*! The priest never caught on, or if he did, he had sense enough not to bother reprimanding us, because it would only have emboldened us to find other phrases to corrupt, perhaps ones that were more crucial to the liturgy and not to be tampered with.

The special wine used on the altar was stored at the residence of the Priest, which was situated about half a mile from the Church. From time to time, one of the altar boys was delegated to go to the residence to get a jar or a bottle of wine for the Church. It became the practice to take the filled bottle or jar and stop at the hill midway between the Priest's residence and the Church where there was a little stream flowing off the Gaze above. Here the boy would take a drink or two of wine and fill the empty space with water. On occasion, it was remarked that the Priest, during Mass, seemed to have a questioning look when he tasted the wine, to which he added water in any case in accordance with the format of the ceremony. It is probable that some boys had a greater liking than others, and the mixture varied accordingly.

Going to confession was always a traumatic occasion for the villagers. Their sins were not great really, but they had grown up believing that all sins were very important, even use of bad language and telling of *"off-colour"* stories, which were more or less commonplace in the village. This, of course, did not put much of a damper on such favoured activities. The majority of men would only go twice a year at most, at Christmas and Easter, and they would not have gone then if they did not feel obliged to do so by the rules of the Church. The confessional was located in the rear of the Church and there would be a long queue on the two obligatory occasions, with a few men grouped in a corner away from the queue jockeying for the last position.

On one such occasion, the Priest had been busy in confessional all afternoon during a heavy thunder and lightning storm and the fury outside seemed to some of the irregulars to be related to their particular sins or perhaps their lengthy and unforgivable absences from the confessional, since the rain had entered and formed large pools on the floor.

One man, who was known to be a bit light-fingered when it came to the possessions of others, was standing in line. It was said of him that they wouldn't trust him with a one-hundred-and-six-pound anchor, because of this tendency of his, so obviously, he had much to confess. And, moreover, he was one of those who put off going to confession and only went when it was an absolute obligation, such as at Easter. Every time someone would come in to go to confession, he would give them his place in line, saying, *"Go ahead, go ahead"* because he was still trying to get up the courage to go in and putting off the inevitable for another few minutes. Finally, there were only two left after the jockeying for the last position and the second last man entered the confessional. As he left, he said to the last man who had joined him as he left the Church, *"Are you going in?"*, to which he replied looking at the pool of water on the floor, *"Jazuz, boy, I think I'll wait until the tide has turned"*!

The majority of the villagers regarded religion and its teachings very seriously and crime of any kind was practically non-existent. There were, however, some exceptions. There were two or three families well known for their dishonesty, of whom it was said *"they'd take the eye out of your head and come back for the hole"*, or *"I wouldn't trust them as far as I could throw them"*.

There was at one time a furnished house that belonged to former residents now living in the US or the mainland of Canada and it stood untouched for years, a tribute to the honesty of the village. At a certain point, however, one or two of the crooks referred to decided to make use of the furnishings, and in a few nights, all things of value were removed. When relatives of the owner complained to the police officer he knew exactly where to go to recover the goods, and he did so, taking two prisoners at the same time.

The prisoners and their loot were brought to the police station on the same wagon and, to the merriment of some residents and the consternation of others, the trip was made accompanied by music provided by the gramophone which they had stolen. All the tunes were sacred, but the favourite played several times during the trip was *"Nearer my God to Thee"*.

The parish priest for many years was an Irishman named Father Sheehan. He was well educated, and sang beautifully, but was very shy, and he had a nervous habit of saying *"Very good, very good"*. It was particularly odd to hear this expression in the confessional after confessing something which one considered a major matter!

As discussed above, some of the old hardliners in the village defied the teachings of the church and didn't go to confession as they were supposed to do at least at Christmas and Easter. So, Father Sheehan preached a particularly vivid sermon of hellfire and brimstone for those who did not observe this obligation one Sunday before Easter and the worst old reprobate was shamed into turning up at the confessional. He was in the confession box at least twenty minutes, having several years of sins to recall and confess and everyone else was forced to wait until he was done, of course, all listening intently, hoping they could overhear some of his offences, most of which were well-known in any event.

All you could hear though, every few minutes was *"Very good, very good"*. When the *"repentant sinner"* finally came out, he had a big smile on his face and he said, *"I must go and sin some more now, I never got so much encouragement in my wandering ways from a priest before as I got from the priest this morning"*!

Earlier I referred to the annual dues which were for the support of the pastor and the fact that in Depression days he often received his dues in kind, or not at all. At that time, it was customary for the Priest to announce each Sunday who had paid and how much, probably as a not too subtle pressure to motivate payment of dues. But other than that, he would not chase after the people to give because he knew how little that they had and, for the most part, that they would give as much as they could afford. So, it wasn't unusual to look in on the priest, as my mother often did, and find him with an overcoat on, because there was no heat in the house, and eating tea and biscuits, because there was nothing else to eat.

One Sunday, Father Sheehan announced a list of contributions in cash, potatoes, beef, fish, labour, etc. and then finished his list with *"and one man, whom I won't mention, gave me a little sheep, but then someone stole the little sheep."* The story behind this statement became known later. Apparently, one of the village minor crooks mentioned earlier felt the pressure enough to make some offering, so one evening he caught a little sheep belonging to someone else and took it to the rectory. He insisted on seeing the Priest to make his donation personally and then asked the Priest where he should put the sheep, that he would come back to slaughter it for him whenever he wanted. The Priest suggested that the barn would be appropriate until he could be sold or butchered, and the man put the animal in the barn and shut the door. He left the yard and returned when he thought the coast was clear and freed the sheep allowing it to rejoin the flock from which he had taken it earlier. This was considered by most of the villagers a scandalous behaviour, but it certainly was an ingenious way to discharge his debt to the Priest without in point of fact committing a mortal sin!

Father Sheehan seemed utterly unaware of time and frequently 9 o'clock Mass would be at 9:30 or 10 or 11; it was never certain. This led to many complaints, but in the main, the flock took it in with good humour and joked about it. His tardiness was such that even midnight Mass on Christmas Eve, which always starts at 12 midnight on the dot, was late on occasion. This led to the following exchange between two of the parishioners: *"What time is midnight Mass tonight"* and the reply *"Towards one o'clock"*.

As the economy improved after the Great Depression, Father Sheehan decided to buy a little car with some money his friends in St. John's gave him to enable him to give better service to the several separate villages which constituted his charge. He had little aptitude as a driver and, in the process of learning, he damaged his gate and garage door on many occasions, although they were wide enough to accommodate a large truck. He was also easily flustered with mechanical things and sometimes, to stop the car, he felt obliged to run into something, hopefully, something soft. In addition, he had the added difficulty of an artificial leg.

One day, as he was leaving to go to another village, he got his artificial leg stuck between the gas pedal and the dashboard and, the more he struggled, the more the pedal depressed and the faster he went. All hands ran for cover as he tried his usual expedient of running into something. He cleared fences on both sides of the road, knocked over horse-carts, scared animals and only succeeded in stopping as he passed the Priest's farm and ran up a hill and up a tree. He remained suspended in the tree with the motor racing until help arrived by foot sometime later. He was unhurt, but he never drove again.

There is, as I have said earlier, a strong streak of impish impiety in Newfoundlanders, although they are basically a religious people, or were so in the period of which I speak. Much of the humour of a situation is, of course, derived from the location and atmosphere which existed at the time and, when an incident occurred in Church, the ordinary became hilarious, particularly for the young.

I remember well one Sunday morning when our family was seated in our double-pew, all ten of us, at the commencement of Mass, and the few usual stragglers made their way to their seats, the centre of all attention.

The pew immediately in front of ours was occupied by an elderly gentleman and his wife and sister. It seems now that they were always late, regardless of the situation, perhaps due to their age. This particular Sunday, the missus came into the Church, up the middle aisle and, as she passed each pew, a sound of suppressed laughter could be heard. When she passed our pew, we quickly saw the reason for the mirth, for attached firmly to the back of her coat was a fish-hook with about four feet of line trailing from it.

My brother, Reg, who was next to me, and who could never seem to whisper and had a deep resonant voice even as a boy, said to me in what he thought was a low voice *"Jeez, look at Mrs. ---, she must have twisted off a troll."* This reference struck a chord in all those who heard, as they were mainly fisher folk who understood the reference and, since he spoke in such a loud voice, about fifty people were soon making strangling sounds with their head down. My father, who had a good sense of humour and laughed long and hard, could not contain himself and had to leave the Church, to the obvious mortification of Mother who turned purple and who saw no humour whatsoever in the situation.

[Editor's Note: It is a common racial stereotype to characterise the Scots as dour and mirthless. Nothing could be further from the truth for "Mom Morry" -- on most occasions. As mentioned previously, before agreeing to raise her children in the RC Church, she had been a member of the United Free Church of Scotland, a particularly stern sect of the Church of Scotland, and no doubt her religious upbringing made this incident all the more scandalous to her.]

Mick Keough
Photo by Stanley Truman Brooks, ca 1935

(The Rooms Corporation, Provincial Archives Division)

On another Sunday, as the latecomers arrived, a little woman known for her toughness and her short temper was rushing to get to her seat while the Priest's back was to the congregation. She was so absorbed in her objective that she ran between the legs of one of the tallest men in the village, who was proceeding in a more leisurely fashion towards his pew. The momentum of the little woman carried the two of them forward several rows before they lost their balance and fell. At this point, as he helped the woman to her feet, the man said: *"Thank you very much, this is as far as I go"*!

The episode was viewed and heard by a large number of parishioners and the laughter and disturbance were such that the Priest delayed the service until conditions became more normal.

In the village, the arrangements for burial were very simple. A local carpenter made a box of suitable size and shape and covered it with a type of cloth and trimming which was readily available in the village stores. The colours were black for old, brown for middle-aged and blue or white for the young and I do not know of any case where this colour scheme did not apply. The only exception would be if a person died elsewhere and was sent home in a casket purchased in the location where he died.

In addition to the coffin, the Convent carried a stack of metal plates on which one of the Sisters would inscribe the name, date of birth and date of death, and this would be fastened to the outside top of the casket. The purpose of this plate was never clear and I do not know anybody who could give a sound reason for it.

On one occasion, a middle-aged man had died and, before he was buried, his widow insisted that she wanted the plate as a memento and it was accordingly removed before the burial. This may have been so at the time she requested it, but a short time later it was put to more practical use. One of the few utensils every family owned was an iron pot, which was used for making stews and soups, baking cakes and bread, making jam and cooking fish. Most of these pots had a cover to start with but, over the years, the covers often were lost or broken and a variety of covers could be seen in use.

The widow's pot cover was the source of amusement to some and horrified gossip to others when it was reported that the plate from the coffin was seen in use on a meal of corned beef and cabbage. One wag who was familiar with the widow's cooking said it was very appropriate, especially the *"Sacred to the Memory of"* and *"RIP"* for he said that the husband was a victim of the worst cooking on the island.

Near the widow's house, there were always pieces of bread, even small loaves on occasion, in the garden or near the road. These were as hard as a rock and nearly black in colour and we boys used to joke about *"Mrs. -----'s hockey pucks"*. I have often wondered if her husband's death had occurred after he had eaten one of these indigestible objects.

After Sunday Mass, there were usually a number of men who came to our house for an hour or so to talk before going home for their dinner. Dinner was always in the middle of the day, especially on Sunday. They generally sat in the kitchen, particularly in fall and winter, as it was the warmest room in the house and, while they talked, the women prepared our meal. The top of the old wood stove was covered with pots and pans with vegetables and other food in them.

Above the kitchen was one of our bedrooms where two of the girls used to sleep, and there was a hatch in the floor to let the heat go upstairs, as there was no heating in the rest of the house. The hatch was usually closed by a sliding door during the day, especially when the bedroom was being cleaned and the beds made up.

This particular Sunday, one of my sisters was "making up" the bed and, as it was quite cool in the room, she opened the hatch to let some heat enter from the kitchen. As she spread the sheet on the bed, one of the others was chasing her around and she inadvertently hit the chamber pot with her foot and upset it. Unfortunately, she had not followed my mother's instructions that before any work was done in a bedroom, the pot was to be emptied, which was the general rule. This sound rule undoubtedly resulted from previous misadventures of the kind. The liquid contents of the pot flowed across the floor and through the hatch onto a red-hot stove and the four or five big pots which covered it. The roast was in the oven with the boiled pudding getting ready and the vegetables in the pot were doing well up to that point. As the stove hissed and the steam rose, nobody said a word, then the company stood as one, suddenly deciding they had somewhere to go and bolted from the room in such a hurry that the last two got jammed in the doorway. None of them said a thing and they were too polite to laugh – until they got outside. The sound of distant laughter could be heard above the angry voice of my mother and the uncontrolled laughter of my father, who never believed in "crying over spilt milk", or spilt urine for that matter.

Needless to say, it was necessary to throw out the food, and the pots had to be scoured and boiled many times before they could be used again. The acrid smell persisted in the kitchen for several days, and my mother insisted that it be repainted. After the event, it was easy to laugh, but at the time of the incident, only the escaped neighbours and my father laughed.

Chapter 3: Childhood Memories

Elsie, Jean, Catherine and Tom Morry on Hay Cart
Photo by Stanley Truman Brooks, ca 1935
(The Rooms Corporation, Provincial Archives Division)

When I was young, our family always had at least two dogs. One was a "setter" or "pointer", which was a hunting dog, and used expressly during the "partridge" season *[Editor's note: "partridge" is what the Willow Ptarmigan is known as in most parts of Newfoundland].* The other was a "water dog", usually a mongrel, part Labrador, used in hunting salt water birds. This dog would plunge into the coldest of water to retrieve birds which could not be picked up except by launching a boat, which was not always possible in the areas where this type of hunting took place. These dogs seemed impervious to cold and, after a swim in the icy water, would shake themselves off and lie down waiting for the next bird to be shot.

Dogs were generally kept in the house, shared the family's food, were loved by the children and, as a result of their treatment, seemed to reach a stage of mental development where they understood much of what was going on around them. To illustrate this, one of our neighbours, one of the older men in the village was a great dog lover and always prided himself on the intelligence of these animals, though it was native to them and not trained into them by him. He had one dog named Spot, that he never let out of his sight except when he went to bed, and maybe not even then.

To prove how intelligent his dog was, one time this man, who live about half a mile from the ocean, would say to his dog *"You need a bath"* and the dog would take off, jump into the water from the wharf, dry himself in the grass and return for his master's inspection. I had seen him do this many times.

He believed that Spot could understand every word he was saying and, when we laughed at him one day when he was telling us this when we were in the woods together cutting wood he said, *"I'll prove it to you"*. He took off his outer trigger mitts (we always wore two pair when working in the woods to save our hands and keep warm) and, when Spot wasn't looking, he hung them by the spring well where we were having a drink.

We headed for home, about five miles away, and when we arrived back at his house he said to Spot, *"Spot, I forgot my mitts"*. Without hesitation Spot headed off back over the trail into the woods and about an hour later, he returned with the mitts in his mouth. That is an absolute fact!

One dog we owned named "Bucky" seemed to understand everything which went on about him and there are those who swore he had a sense of humour and was a practical joker. At that time many people made their own beer and liquor, and molasses was a basic ingredient. It was also a basic item of diet substituting on occasion for more expensive items of groceries such as butter and sugar. My family kept a small general store, and when someone wanted molasses, it was necessary to draw it from a puncheon with the container being a pail which the customer provided.

One day, a local widow who helped out her meagre pension by making and selling beer sent a neighbour to buy some molasses. After he obtained the molasses, he stopped to speak to a passerby and, during the conversation which lasted for several minutes, he left the pail near him on the ground.

Bucky passed by, inspected the pail, looked to see if he was being watched, lifted his leg and increased the contents of the pail. This was seen by the other man, who always swore that Bucky had a big smile on his face as he hurried away. He said nothing of the incident and in due course, the beer was made and he promptly christened it "Bucky's ale". He did not give any explanation until long after the beer was consumed, but ever after the beer made by the woman was always known by the brand name he had bestowed.

Another day, a visitor arrived at our home with a beautiful new car accompanied by his girlfriend. This man was generally welcome except that, when he was drinking, he was somewhat obnoxious. The visitor knew my mother would not like to see him in this state but he decided to drop in for a few moments to see what the situation would be, leaving both car doors open, as he did not expect to be long.

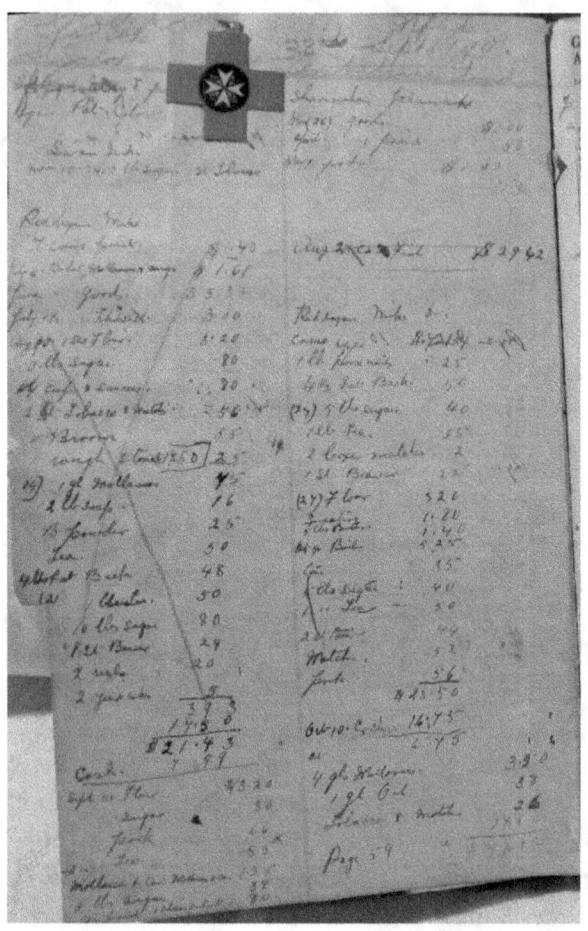

Page from Howard Morry's shop ledger showing suspiciously large orders of molasses
Photo by the editor
Ledger now deposited with Provincial Archives Division, The Rooms

Bucky seemed to sense the atmosphere and mood of my mother for he left the house, inspected the car, lifted his leg by the driver's seat and urinated, and then walked around the car and gave the same treatment to the passenger seat. When the visitor and his companion left rapidly and in a huff at my mother's invitation, they jumped in the car and those who were watching saw clearly a look of astonishment on each face as they drove off. In the meantime, Bucky was sitting near the road, laughing heartily, or so it is believed to this day.

When I was in my teens, each village had at least one home where the young gathered each night to play cards, joke, sing songs and gossip. The house of one man, whom I came to think of as a sort of *"philosopher"*, was one of our favourite places to spend the evenings, and our parents were happy to let us visit there. He and his wife never seemed to mind how many of us were crowded into the kitchen playing cards, telling jokes and carrying on, as youngsters always did and still do.

One evening around Christmas-time, while the man of the house was out scouting the village for some moonshine and sampling the various vintages his neighbours made, his wife washed the floor. She used the same pan for this purpose that she used to bake bread and many other kitchen uses and when she was done, she went to the door and threw out the water but forgot to rinse the pan. When her husband came home dancing, with his eyes glistening from the moonshine, he announced to the wife that he would have a shave, an occasion of rare occurrence, except on a Sunday morning. Nevertheless, to humour him she boiled some water and forgetfully put it in the same pan she had just washed the floor with. When he was finished shaving, there was more stuff sticking on his face than the beard he started with, bits of paper, fish bones and offal, and all kinds of other dirt from the floor, but in the state he was in, he didn't seem to notice, though the rest of us were splitting our sides. It was sure a sight to see; it was almost incredible that someone would do that.

For all her good points, and there were many, putting up with the likes of us being foremost, this dear woman was not much of a cook. One thing she never did seem to master was bread making, though every other woman in every house in the village seemed to have mastered the skill. The family put up with it, but they didn't go through much flour, as the end result was effectively inedible. One time when she was sick, her husband asked their neighbour to bake some bread for his family. The neighbour was well-known in the village for the quality of her baked goods, and the beautiful brown crusty bread was no sooner presented to the children than it vanished instantly. So, he gave her more flour and ingredients and asked her to make more bread for the next day, and it vanished in the same manner. This went on for several days and finally, he had to say to her, *"Can you try not to make your bread so good; the children are eating me out of house and home."* Unfortunately for him and fortunately for the boys, she would have none of it and he had to put up with his boys devouring her bread until he could find someone in the village whose bread was more like that of his wife and then things got back to normal and he was saved from bankruptcy.

People on the Southern Shore, in the best tradition of the Irish, had a way of using words that was not common to everybody. For instance, they would use the word "wonderful" in two senses; they'd use in the good sense, that something wonderful was going to happen; but they would also use it instead of "terrible" on occasion, or for another word of similar meaning. For example, it's not funny really, but it's an example of how this happened and how this second sense was used. Two men, a father and his son, were lost on a small schooner, unfortunately, an all too common occurrence in outport Newfoundland. The word reached the villagers in Aquaforte, where they resided and the women got together and decided to go over and see the wife of the family and give her the bad news in as gentle a manner as possible before she heard of it some other way. So, they went along and went up to her door. The spokeswoman said *"Hey, Mrs. -----."* "Yes?" *"Prepare yourself for a wonderful surprise; your husband and son were drowned yesterday."*

Often there were practical jokers in the gathering and their activities were sometimes hilarious, but usually only to those who perpetrated them.

In Depression days, those who had a little more than others usually donated some of their goods to the less fortunate. For example, if someone killed a cow or bull for their own use, the head would normally be given to a poor family for soup, the heart and liver to another. Once, when my father killed a steer, he sent me off with the head and the liver to the house where we spent many of our evenings to thank them for putting up with us.

The gift was received with gratitude and the liver was immediately cooked and the head prepared for the inevitable pot of soup. With a mess of vegetables, the head would make a pot of soup that would do for a week for all hands. On this occasion, I didn't have time to clean the head so I took it over, eyeballs, horns, nostrils and all as it was, just the skin off of it. I said, *"Sorry sir I only had time to skin it, I've got to go down the shore with my father."*

That evening, when we arrived at the house as usual for a game of cards, a large pot was boiling merrily on the stove, a nice smell around, and, from time to time, throughout the evening, some onions, spices and vegetables were added, apparently in preparation for a midnight scoff. At one point someone lifted the lid off the pot and looking up out of it was a set of eyeballs and the short horns were still on there. What a shock that was!

Another night, there had been some drinking and, as there was a snow-storm, there was a crowd there. It was warm and comfortable, with the old Waterloo stove blazing away, and there was a friendly and welcoming atmosphere. One of the party, who was a bit of a hell-raiser, and who lived some distance away, had too much to drink and was asked to stay for the night on the sofa in the kitchen. During the evening, the missus had made bread and, on occasion, as it rose, she punched it down and placed a cloth over the pan on the bread and an old coat on top of that to keep the bread warm during the night. There was no central heating, of course, and, since the kitchen fire was always allowed to die during the night, the foregoing precaution was necessary. Since there was someone who would be staying during the night and the fire would presumably be kept going, the pan of dough was placed on a chair at some distance from the stove to avoid undue expansion of the dough.

When she had gone to bed, one of the lads (I'm not about to reveal which one, though I will admit I was always good at science), understanding the chemistry of bread-making, unobtrusively placed the chair holding the dough nearer the stove just before he left, and nobody seemed to notice.

After we had gone, the household members retired for the night and the guest stoked the fire, put out the lights and lay down. He woke once or twice and added wood to the fire, but then he settled down and, as he had had much to drink, he fell sound asleep. This unwanted heat of course eventually caused the bread dough to rise and overflow the pan.

Towards dawn, the cold woke him and he glowered in the gloom toward the stove. To his horror, he saw what he thought was a grey face with a black coat moving towards him on the floor. He closed his eyes, thinking he was suffering *"D. T.s"*, which indeed he had experienced about a year before. He thought about it for a few minutes and looked again, only to find in absolute terror that the apparition with the ominous black cloak was now even closer to him. He had not undressed the night before, except for removing his sea-boots. He now stealthily located and donned his boots, seized his coat and hat and bolted from the house at top speed.

It was some time before he again visited the house and when he did, he related his experience to much hilarity on the part of those present. Nobody explained the circumstances to him and it is likely that to this day he thought that he saw a supernatural apparition. His explanation of what he saw, given without embellishment, was one of the most amusing stories I have ever heard.

The kitchen stove had an oven below for baking and another above for heating or warming. The top oven was rarely used, except for keeping a plate warm for a latecomer.

One evening, when we were sitting around playing cards, one of the household rose to stoke the fire with wood and, when he opened the door of the stove, distant strains of music could be heard. The stoker dropped the door of the stove and most of those present looked apprehensively at the stove door, but the music stopped as soon as the door closed. The immediate reaction was that something supernatural had occurred, and several of those present crossed themselves, and some prayed.

After a few minutes, someone suggested that the fire would go out unless it was fed, but at first, nobody wanted to go near the stove. Finally, my brother Bill, who was always a doubter of the supernatural, volunteered to put some wood in the stove and, accordingly, he chose a couple of billets and lifted the door.

Again, there was the unmistakable sound of music and he dropped the door without inserting the wood. Soon afterwards there was a general exodus of visitors and the family decided to spend the night at a neighbour's, and to have the Priest in the next day to examine the stove and take the necessary steps to use the power of the Church to expel the devil who by now was thought to inhabit the stove.

Next day, the Priest came and the family entered very timidly. They explained what happened and he, noting the seriousness of the family, said a few prayers before he opened the stove door. This time there was no music and the family thought and probably believe to this day that the supernatural forces had been banished by the Priest.

Sometime later, the phenomenon was explained by the perpetrator of the hoax (far be it from me to take credit for this clever stunt). He had placed a small radio in the top oven with a thin wire lead to the inside of the stove door, which he had attached when he had risen early in the evening during the card game to put some wood in the stove. The lead activated the radio by switching it on or off when the door was opened or closed. He had taken the radio out during the confusion involved in the general exodus.

One of the fishermen in Ferryland married a girl from outside, I don't know where she came from, I think she probably belonged to St. John's, but she was a little more refined and accomplished as a homemaker than most of the village women, who were dragged out from raising kids and having less than enough to cook with most of the time. She was always making him special dainty cakes and so on. When he'd go out on the fishing ground with his mates and it came to lunchtime, all the other boys would boil up the fish and potatoes and haul out the homemade bread that they had and make a good meal of it. But he was always pulling out something like *"blancmange"* and things like that, the names of which he had learned from his wife and never heard before.

One time when he was out and it came lunchtime, he joined his mate for the fish but then pulled out some dainty little cookies and offered them to him. His dory mate declined, and he seemed to be a little put out about it. This guy's wife was a notoriously bad cook. Finally, to finish up the man with the *"foreign"* wife took out a delicate piece of pound cake and said to his mate, *"Well then, will you have a piece of this nice pound cake"*. And the other fella pulled out of his bag some kind of odd-looking duff and cut it with his gutting knife and said: *"No boy, I got one here a pound and a half."*

When we were growing up in Ferryland, my mother usually had a maid who was commonly a girl from one of the local families or sometimes from a nearby village. I remember one of them came to work for us after having worked for another family in Ferryland previously. The reason she was there was that the old man was in his late years and he had no one who belonged to the family to look out for him and the boys paid her to go down and clean the house once in a while and cook a meal for him. One day, she was standing in the kitchen cooking a bit of food for the old man's breakfast. It was a fine day, but when she looked out, coming past the window there was a lot of water. She couldn't think what was happening but she paid no attention because she was busy.

Next day, the same time, the same thing happened and, about this time, she started connecting it with the time the old man got out of bed. He used to get out of bed at about 9:30 or 10 o'clock and when he got up this usually happened. Well, there was no indoor plumbing in 99% of the houses in outport Newfoundland back then. Most of them had a privy and those that didn't used a chamber pot in which people did whatever they had to do. About the third or fourth time this happened she went outside and looked up and here was the old man with his thing-a-ma-jig laid on the sill of the window and he was quietly taking a leak down the side of the house. As she looked up, she realised that the white paint on the side of the house was steadily getting darker and darker with a yellow tinge. So, she was wondering what she was going to do about it. There was no good in speaking to the old man; a) he'd deny it, and b) he'd tell her to mind her own business. She figured there had to be some way to settle that up if that was the case.

So, the next morning, the minute she saw the very first drop coming down, she went out with the broom and she hit the broom hard on the side of the house to let the old man know he had been detected. It was a frame house, as all the houses were in the village and a very flimsy structure. And when the broom shook the side of the house, the window dropped, and she heard an ear-piercing scream from up above, and sure enough, there was the old man, cursing at having been discovered. I'm not sure whether that put an end to it, but it did put an end to her employment in that family!

Another one of the maids that we had came over from somewhere in St. Mary's Bay. She came to us late in the year when our mother was in the hospital, as she was many times with a bad sinus condition that led to numerous operations. My father brought in a goose for Christmas, in the old British tradition rather than a turkey in the North American tradition – an innovation introduced to the family by our Scottish mother. So, on Christmas Eve my father brought in the goose. Of course, it was intact and it had to be gutted and plucked and so on. He was going out and the rest of us were put to bed.

As soon as the house quietened down, the maid decided to take the goose and get it ready. So, she picked it up apparently, and got to work and started to pluck it. She hadn't gone very far when the goose let out a loud honk. She threw the goose in the middle of the floor and climbed on the table and that is where my father, coming home sometime after midnight, found her. She was still standing on the table with a look of abject terror on her face. In the middle of the floor was the goose, partially plucked.

He said, *"My God! What happened to you?"* She said, *"Take that thing away, it's still alive."* He said, *"It can't be alive, its been dead for two weeks."* But she insisted it was alive and he had to take it away. So, he took and put it on the back porch and came back in and she was still crouched on the table. He began to interrogate her as to exactly what happened. She said, *"I had just begun to pluck that thing and when I got to the wing the pin feathers were hard to remove so I gave it a great pull and the minute I did the goose gave a great honk, so I threw it in the middle of the floor because it was alive."*

Of course, what really happened was that there had gotten to be some gas in the bird as it was hanging and ageing and, when she pulled hard, she forced the air out of the mouth of the bird and made a sound something like a honk. But she was superstitious enough that, on a dark night and all on her own, she could easily believe that the goose had come back to life!

In the early days of radio, it was quite an event to listen to voices and music from far away, even if they were frequently interrupted and sometimes blanked by static. Very few people had radios and an invitation to listen to the radio was much prized. I remember my first experience of this kind was at my Uncle John's when I was permitted a turn with the earphones.

[Editor's Note: On the 1935 Census, the question was asked if there was a radio in the household. Dad's father did not own one. But his brother, John, did. By 1945, this question was no longer asked. Instead, the question that stood out was whether there had been TB in the household. Signs of the changing times.]

As radio developed and more people managed to buy a set, it became a veritable lifeline in the outports of Newfoundland, particularly in winter when communication by land or water were often shut down. People used the service programmes to send messages to other villagers regarding joyous occasions, sickness, disasters, and deaths as well. Reports on patients hospitalized in St. John's were also given, as were notices of upcoming marriages and births. About that time the *"all request"* programme began developing and a new form of amusement was born. It wasn't long before listeners began requesting selections for other people, often without guile, but frequently in a mischievous way to chronicle some local happening. The poor announcers in St. John's, not being up to date on the comings and goings and the scandals on the Southern Shore, were often unwitting accomplices to some devilment on the part of the requestors.

In the village there was one gossip, a cousin of mine, who was well-known for her interest in other people's affairs to the extent that, occasionally, if there was a gathering in a home, she would, under cover of darkness, position herself near a window to ascertain the subject of conversation. She picked up many a juicy piece of gossip in this way. She became known for this practice and it was only a short while before the announcer on the *"all request"* programme read a letter requesting a song entitled *"Under your window tonight"* requested for *"Miss ----"* – by her friends. Everyone in the village listened to the programme and everyone, including knew the reason for the selection. I do not know if this cured her, but I know she was never caught in that situation afterward.

There was also an amorous triangle of which all were aware. A woman on the south side of the harbour had a husband but rarely shared the marital bed with him, and probably never even ate with him. But he wasn't around much anyway; he used to be out playing cards or what have you. And when he was out, she had not one but two suitors, one married, one single. I'm not sure how they knew when the husband was gone or, for that matter, when the other suitor wasn't already there before they went "visiting", whether by smoke signal or what, to know that the coast was clear to go there.

The favoured man varied from time to time, but then the woman concerned seemed to have made a choice and, for some months, the married man was a frequent visitor at her home. The less favoured suitor knew of the other man and was very jealous of him. So, when he'd go up, if he saw the tracks of the other guy going in, he'd go away pretty angry about it. Eventually, he said to himself, *"I'm going to fix that so-and-so."*

He went in one night early, and he backed into the house leaving footprints in the fresh snow that made it look like whoever had been there had left and the coast was clear. And then he waited behind the porch with a bloody great stick in his hands until the other guy showed up. So, *"John"*, I'll call him, showed up, looked over the fence, saw the steps were in the right direction and proceeded to go to the door. Just as he was about to open the door, Jack, I'll call him, came out from behind the porch and hit him so hard with the stick that he landed halfway back to the gate and *"Jack"* took off out of there before *"John"* came to.

That seemed to end his affection for the married woman and he never came back. But the tide had turned, and now *"Jack"* seemed to have the inside track. This generated a request for a song entitled *"Back in the saddle again"* for *"Jack ----"*. This was the source of much amusement in the village.

Nobody knew what was going to come on that programme but anyone who had any foible or had been caught doing anything they shouldn't have been doing soon found themselves on the winning end of a request from Ferryland on the *"all requests"* programme.

Ferryland Harbour and Isle au Bois
Photo by the editor, 1974

Another despondent suitor used the programme to advertise his affections with a request for *"Lover come back to me"*. Many and varied were the requests and a wide variety of significant items were chronicled in this fashion. The days of radio will always be remembered with nostalgia by those who lived in the outports of Newfoundland in the period concerned.

One of the villagers was always complaining of his lot to all and sundry. He was so well-known as a bore and a nuisance that people used to hide when they saw him coming, but he was usually able to find some kinder person to listen to his tale of woe. According to him, he was the most unfortunate man in the world. His wife was a banshee, his children did not respect him, he never caught any fish, his boat was leaky, his nets were torn, his garden was poor, and everything, even God, was against him.

He spent most of his time complaining, and this, of course, left little time for improving his lot. His nets were the last in the water, his garden was the last planted, and the results of his efforts were therefore usually less than the results obtained by his neighbours. This was explainable, but he would never listen to a word of advice or counsel.

One cold, cold day in spring, some of the more industrious fishermen were working repairing their nets and were unable to escape when the malcontent came along. He chose as his target one of the hardest working men in the village who, like many other fishermen, had spent some time in the *"Boston States"* fishing out of Gloucester when the fish were scarce at home. He came back again when things were improved a bit. He married and had sons and they fished together and always did well at the fishery and his gardens produced well because of their hard work.

The grumbler started comparing his results with that of the *"Yankee"* and began telling him how lucky he was to get such good results. He complained that he had no money to get gear to go fishing, his boat had a hole in it, his family was sick, he wasn't feeling very well himself, and so on. He went on and on, not pausing for comment, and not listening when one was offered, until he finally said, *"I believe I'll end it all; if I had a piece of rope, I'd hang myself"*. Fed up with his complaining, and willing to help him to achieve his wish, the other man replied quickly, *"Here boy, take the whole coil"* and handed him 50 fathoms of rope. That was the end of the pest for that day at least.

When I was young, the fishery was vigorously prosecuted, and every able-bodied man in the village took part in this industry. It was most unusual for a fisherman to be paid wages; in almost all cases the men fished together as "sharemen" or "co-adventurers". In the case of fishermen who used trolls, each of the two who fished together owned an equal number of trolls or they owned them jointly. In the case of trap fishing, the usual arrangement was for the skipper to own the traps and the boat and to get two shares for himself if he was a member of a crew. Each of the latter got a share each. Costs of operating the boat, purchasing salt, fuel, etc., were shared in the same fashion.

During most of the years of my youth, my father fished actively as skipper, but after an illness, he was obliged to ease up, and a member of the crew was designated as skipper. During my last years in the village, Mick Keough *[Editorial Note: his real name]* was the skipper.

He was a man of infinite good humour and optimism. When there was no fish, he always expected there would be plenty after the wind changed, or on the change of the tides. He was not always right, but the number of times he was right far outweighed the few times he was wrong, and it was easier to forget the latter. He was well-liked among the young fellas in Ferryland and he spent much time with them because he had lost his own son, who was the exact same age as my brother, to a mysterious illness just before his teens. He always hung around us when we were down on the wharf to make sure we were alright.

Phonse Kavanagh's crew at the trap
Photo by the editor, 1969

Mick was well regarded by the crew, but they frequently played tricks on him in an affectionate manner. One morning, all hands were in the boat except Mick, who hurried down the pier to get aboard the skiff. As he did so, one of the lads pushed the skiff away from the wharf and Mick stepped into about twelve feet of water. He could swim and was in no danger and was soon pulled aboard, thoroughly wet and a little angry, but he was not angry about being wet. Unfortunately, as he hit the cold water the shock caused his mouth to open and his bottom denture dropped into the water. He had the worst set of false teeth you ever saw in your life; they were all exactly the same size and they were all made out of china. We used to call them "China Clippers". Teeth like those were common in Newfoundland in those days and they were always falling out so most people left them in their pocket, most of the time, or on the dresser. They no more fitted him than the man in the moon, but nevertheless, they were an expense he could ill-afford and he would not be able to replace them. Besides that, Mick liked the way he looked with them!

Great excitement ensued when he announced his loss and all present scanned the bottom to see where the dentures lay. Eventually, someone spied them near a large rock, where they gleamed in the rays of the sun. Mick became a good deal less agitated when he saw that his dentures were apparently safe and sound, and he was about to leave to change his wet clothes when he saw first one and then another sculpin approaching slowly towards the dentures.

The sculpin is a scavenger with a very large mouth and he is always prepared to eat anything he sees and is particularly attracted to anything shiny. The sculpins stopped about a foot away from the dentures, opening and closing their mouths, moving towards the prize, and moving away as the tide ebbed and flowed, while Mick, in the boat, swore and yelled. He said, *"Jazuz, Jazuz, try and keep those sculpins away."*

Eventually, someone ran to the beach for stones to drop, but Mick objected lest his dentures be broken in the process. Then someone hit on the idea of catching the sculpins with a cod jigger, and this was agreed to by Mick. As soon as the jigger was lowered, more sculpins came quickly out of the deep and, although a number were caught, they were replaced by at least as many others, which seemed to be bigger and more voracious than those which were caught.

By this time, Mick was so excited that he slipped and fell into the water and had to be pulled out again. For the moment, the dentures were forgotten, and when they looked again, they were gone. Mick was now so agitated that he was almost speechless, and when the boat moved in the wind, he was even more disturbed to see that the dentures were now being nosed by a large sculpin, who had apparently already tasted them and was contemplating swallowing them. One of the crew used the boat hook, which is a long pole with a hook on the end, to scare the sculpin away, and a council was held to decide how the dentures were to be recovered.

At first, a small hook on a line was used. It was necessary to manoeuvre the hook gently near the dentures and then lift them slowly towards the surface. Several times the first part of the procedure was successful and all hands held their breath as the dentures were slowly lifted towards the surface, but each time, when they got up to where the tide was heavier, they fell from the hook, and slowly sank, glittering as they turned over and over on their journey to the bottom, where perhaps a dozen rapacious sculpin were now gathered.

Mick was by now in such a state that he was interfering with the rescue attempts, so he was led away with some pressure, as well as persuasion, by the senior member of the crew.

After Mick's departure, in a calmer atmosphere, the remaining members of the crew pondered the problem and devised a scheme to complete the rescue. This consisted simply of the hook and line mentioned earlier and a dip-net, which is a net with a long handle. The handle was lengthened by joining it to the handle of the boat-hook. The dentures were lifted off the bottom and, as soon as they were about six feet from the surface, the net was slipped underneath, and the dentures were recovered, none the worse for the adventure.

They were returned to Mick as quickly as possible and his happiness was evidenced by an offer of a drink to all hands to celebrate the recovery. He was very grateful and was heard to say, *"By the Jeez, I was some lucky to get them teeth back. If you hadn't been successful, I would have had to spend the rest of the summer jigging sculpins, I wouldn't have gone fishing at all until I found my teeth."*

One of the village families was boiling a meal of salt beef for Sunday dinner. The way salt beef was then sold, it had a string in through it to hold it together, and neither the husband who brought the meat home nor his wife who cooked it remembered to take the string out when the meat was put in the pot. She boiled it as it was, piling the greens on top of it - dandelions and so on - and everybody was looking forward to this beautiful meal.

Anyway, finally, it got put on the table. So, the wife tucked into what was going to a great meal and she was eating with much gusto Next thing, the husband says, *"What's hanging out of your mouth there?"* and he reached over and got hold of a piece of string and started hauling on it, she swallowed the stuff and everything and he's hauling and he hauled about six feet of line out of her and he said, *"Jazuz, you're ravelling out!"*. The rest of us were running for the door trying to keep from laughing so we wouldn't be accused of laughing at her.

In the next village lived a very industrious woman who, in addition to keeping house, cooking, and helping with the fish curing, knitted sweaters, gloves, etc., for anyone who would buy them. Since there was always some wife ill, and a certain number of bachelors without close relatives, there was generally a market for her products.

There was only one problem with her products: she would sometimes lose count, and she used her judgement to decide on the number of stitches she had left to go in the pattern rather than unravel the item and start again. This was bad enough when she was knitting a sweater, which might turn out too long, too short, too wide, or too narrow since she never took any measurements. When, however, the project was gloves, the results were often ludicrous, one long one, one short, one wide, one narrow, etc.

I remember one year when my mother was ill in hospital Dad commissioned this lady to knit a sweater for him and several pair of gloves for him and the children. She was a fast worker and, about two weeks after receiving the order, she appeared at the house with the finished products. My father paid her the agreed amount and, when she departed, we tried on the gloves and my father put on the sweater.

When we looked at one another, some of the children began to cry and the others began to laugh. My father laughed so hard he had to sit down. His sweater was far too short; there was a space of about six inches between his belt and the bottom of the sweater. In addition, it was so wide that it was big enough for two men as big as my father, although he was over six feet tall and weighed 250 pounds. Finally, one sleeve stopped just below the elbow, while the hand on the other side was covered by the sleeve. The gloves in every case were of two sizes but, by examining all of the so-called pairs, it was possible to rearrange them into better-matched pairs. When my mother returned from the hospital and saw the sweater and gloves, she immediately unravelled them and started knitting and, with the help of some friends, we eventually got garments which fitted properly. This was the last order this particular lady received from my family. We applauded her industry but did not buy her products.

We always had cats when we were growing up – and dogs – but Elsie, one of my sisters, loved cats dearly and she used to smuggle her favourite up to her bed with her. As a rule, the cats were kept in the barn or in the kitchen. One of the cats was very, very pregnant and my mother was saying to her, *"Don't take that cat upstairs."* But she didn't know how to tell her why Elsie being quite young at the time and having yet been exposed to the *"facts of life"*. So, one morning Elsie went down to the kitchen and got the cat to bring it up in the bed with her, and the cat was already in labour. As she brought it into the bed, squeezing it and hugging it, a stream of kittens came out of the cat onto the bed and my mother saw it all and was horrified and had to explain prematurely to a little girl how this all came about and how the cat happened to have a belly full of kittens. A practical lesson in the birds and the cats you might say!

In the old days, every schooner, brig and other sailing ship had on board a small canon about three or four feet long. This was not for defence, as it would have been useless for that purpose. It was actually a safety device used to identify the location of the vessel when approaching the shore in a dense fog, a climatic condition almost always present on the Southern shore through the spring and summer months. The peal of the canon would not only prevent two vessels from colliding with one another in the fog, but the echo of the stony headlands would give some indication of the relative closeness to shore.

We had one of these little brass canons in the house when I was growing up. I can only assume that it was a holdover from an earlier generation when many Morrys were ship's masters as well as vessel owners.

One day my brother Reg and I decided it was high time to put this canon to the test. We snuck it out of the house and out to the end of the stage where we secured it with rope to the heading table pointing out over the harbour. There was always plenty of powder and shot around because, like in every house, most of the boys were fond of hunting and refilled their own shotgun shells. So, we loaded the little canon with what we thought was a reasonable charge, put in some lead shot for effect. and wadded it down with an old rag we found lying around.

Then it came time to decide who would be brave enough to ignite this *"weapon"*. A game of *"rock, scissors, hammer"* decided the matter and Reg *"won"*! He put a little powder in the hole, lit a match and gingerly approached the cannon. No sooner had he gotten within an inch of the hole, the power ignited and the cannon went off with a deafening roar that would certainly have been heard all the way to the southside of the harbour. Unfortunately, the intensity of the blast caused the poorly tied ropes to give a little and, rather than firing out high over the harbour, the muzzle turned downward and emptied its full charge through the side of a skiff anchored just off the end of the wharf. We didn't stick around to know the rest of the story. We were probably halfway to Calvert by the time the skiff sank to the bottom. But there was no escaping who was responsible, and you can bet that in the end, we did pay the penalty.

In the village, there was no official barber, but there were a number of unofficial barbers who would cut hair for free or for a small gratuity. It was the usual practice to arrange the time for a hair-cut and to go to the barber's house at the appointed time. The usual gratuity was a plug of tobacco or a pack of cigarettes. The problem of a barber getting a haircut himself was usually settled by exchange service with other unofficial barbers.

The haircuts had a monotonous similarity; no matter what one said to the barber, the cut was the same. No attempt was made to shape the hair; it was shortened, doused with water and combed, and no complaints were expected or made.

One of the barbers was a small man with a very quick temper. Although he was small, nobody in the village would tangle with him. One day he cut a neighbour's hair on the exchange basis, having been told that the neighbour had given many haircuts.

On the day *"John"*, I'll call him, was to get his haircut in exchange, his neighbour offered to come to his house to do the job and, although this was unusual, John agreed, because it was more convenient for him. After the usual small talk, John seated himself in a kitchen chair and the haircut commenced.
For a while, all seemed to be going well, the scissors snipped, the hair fell and the conversation continued. Then the snipping

stopped and *"Pat"* (as good a name as any), the neighbour, turned John around in the chair so that his back was to the small mirror on the wall and began snipping here and there in a somewhat random fashion. John was beginning to wonder what was going on when Pat said, *"Stay there while I get a drink"* and went into the kitchen to get a drink of water. John heard the door open and close and then the back door banged shut and John heard running footsteps in the lane.

He rose and was surprised to see Pat running down the lane as fast as he could go. John wondered why until he looked in the mirror and then he knew. His hair was almost completely gone on one side and the other side was jagged, some places long, some short. The back was up to his crown on one side and untouched on the other. John was furious. He couldn't follow Pat with his hair as it was, but he made a fervent vow to pay him back somehow as soon as possible.

John waited until dark and went to the house of another barber who collaborated with him in making the best of the situation. It was necessary to cut off most of his hair and he wore a cap day and night until his hair had grown out again.

In the meantime, Pat avoided John and the latter bided his time. He knew that Pat normally got his hair cut by *"Harry"*, let's say, who was away at sea, and he would be returning home soon. When Harry returned, John made an arrangement with him that he would be notified of the time of Pat's next haircut and, one Saturday, Harry told him Pat would be at his house for a haircut at 5:00 PM. John went to Harry's just before 5:00 and, when Pat arrived, Harry sat him in a chair with the back to the door of the room where John was hidden and excused himself for a moment. Immediately, John slipped into the room silently and replaced Harry. With a pair of clippers, he made a cut from the middle of the back to the middle of the front and another from ear to ear. At this stage, he announced his presence and passed the hand mirror to Pat, who almost fainted when he saw a white cross on his black, wavy head of hair.

He tried to persuade the barbers to make some kind of repairs to enable him to go on a date that night, but nobody would do anything, and in fact, it is doubtful if anybody could do anything. For several weeks Pat wore a cap to cover the cross, but the entire village was in on the prank and ingenious methods were employed to knock off the cap and expose the cross. Pat, who was normally a good church-goer, did not appear at church for several Sundays in spite of the urgings of the Priest because he would have been forced to doff his hat. Pat never cut hair again.

Cars were very rare on the Southern Shore in Depression Days and, if a car was heard up on the road, we'd all rush up there to have a look at it. One of my friends was walking down the main road through the village one day and came upon a man standing beside a car with the hood up and swearing. Not having seen an automobile close up before, he stopped to see what the man was about. The driver told him that he had run out of gasoline and asked him if would go to the store and bring him back some gasoline. My friend was very obliging and wanted to help the poor stranger, so he agreed to do this.

Gas was cheap then, and the man gave him a twenty-five-cent piece and told him to have something for himself for his trouble out of the change. He probably wanted to get about a half-gallon of gas, about ten cents or so, enough for him to drive the car to where he could fill it. Anyway, my friend went to the only store in the village that had gasoline and started by asking for a plug of Beaver tobacco which was 24 cents. Strictly speaking, we were not supposed to smoke or chew. But what the folks didn't know wouldn't hurt them, we figured. When he was done and had given the shopkeeper the twenty-five-cents he suddenly remembered the gasoline he had come to get and asked the shop keeper, *"Could I have the rest of the worth of it in gas"*. The shop keeper put the money in the cash register, rang up the sale and took him to a can of gasoline and said, *"Dip your finger in there, then we'll be square."*

Mom Morry's car outside of the Morry store, ca 1935
Morry Family Collection

I don't know what happened to the motorist, but my friend panicked and didn't know what to do, so he ran off in the opposite direction to the car. It wasn't that he was dishonest and meant to take the man's money, but he couldn't count and didn't know the value of things, and was flustered when he learned there wasn't enough left to buy the gasoline. But, on the bright side, he had tobacco enough for a week.

Chapter 4: Characters

In every village there was a place where the men hung out, maybe a couple of places. In Ferryland, one of them was the forge, where two Johnston brothers, Charlie and Nick *[Editor's note: These are their real names; no point trying to hide them – there was only one forge in the village!]*, shoed the horses. Pretty near every house on the shore at that time had a horse or two because they used to haul out wood and they needed a horse for haying and hauling fertilizer for crops, and for hauling the crops home.

And so, as a young boy, this was the place to go. And to justify being there, and to be able to eavesdrop on the stories being told, some of which my mother would be shocked to think I heard, I would offer to pump the bellows. But nonetheless, the stories were harmless, in a way. Nick was a comical soul who always had an answer for anything anyone ever said to him. It was said he was also one of the greatest liars unhung! Not a harmful liar, a liar who tells stories, and therefore an important addition to the village entertainment.

My uncle John was like that too, and in direct competition with Nick. They would vie with one another to tell stories that would top the other one. One day I was there, Nick was telling a story about a man in the village (I'll call him Tom) who got a thorn in his hand when he was working on the Southern Shore railroad that was going in at the time. Nick said he was hoping to get a pension because of it! But in any case, he didn't attend to it well and the finger never bent again, and he had that arm in slings for weeks and weeks but the finger never did heal properly, and thus he had a straight finger thereafter, all gnarled and worn. Strange to say, in the end, he did get a little pension, enough to buy a little tobacco.

*The short-lived Southern Shore Railway
Ferryland Downs and Lighthouse in the Background
Canadian Science and Technology Museum*

But he always had the damn thing wrapped up in yards and yards and yards of white rag. One day around the forge, they were talking about the importance of having a good drawing chimney built in a certain way to draw properly and Nick said: *"I have the best drawing chimney in the village."* Uncle John said, *"That's nothing, I've got one draws so hard you can barely stand in the same room."* To which Nick, not wanting to be outdone, said, *"Jazuz that's nothing, Tom was up to the house the other night and we had the brick out of the chimney to clean out the flue. Tom started unwrapping his finger to show the wife, and unbeknownst to him the end of the rag was going up the chimney and the rag was nearly off when it took myself and William and the wife all our strength to keep Tom from going up the chimney."* Of course, everyone was laughing but Nick insisted, *"Stop laughing, it's the truth, I would never tell a lie about a thing like that!"*

My uncle John was nearly as bad, if not worse. One day he was telling a bunch of men waiting for the tide to turn to go fishing

"You know, I nearly lost my mother last night." Someone fell for it and said, *"That's awful John, what happened?"* John said, *"We've got an alarm clock over there and I set the alarm clock for her and came over and gave it to her and she had on a long nightdress and she started up the stairs and somehow she triggered the alarm. The alarm went off and the key caught in her nightdress and started winding it up and, when I went up to help, all as I could hear were muffled sounds and she was lying on the floor with her eyes protruding. The goddam alarm clock had wound her nightdress all the way up around her neck like a rope. In another second she would have been gone."*

Of course, everyone listening was going *"Ha, ha, ha"*. But uncle John said *"Jeez, you don't believe me?"*, he'd get right angry when people wouldn't fall for one of his tall tales hook, line and sinker.

Another day, he was telling people about the time three years before he was mowing hay in the Barkhouse Meadow, a big field near his house, and he said, *"You know I was mowing the Barkhouse up there that time and it was getting hot, so I hove off my vest and I never found it again afterwards. We killed a cow yesterday"* he said, *"and the local butcher did the killing for me. When we opened her up, here was a part of me vest right up by the heart with my pocket watch in the pocket. Not only that, it had only lost about three minutes in all those three years, the movement of the heart kept it wound up all the time."* Of course everyone was laughing and that got him mad again, *"Don't laugh at what I'm telling you, it's the God's truth, if you don't believe me go ask the butcher."* of course the butcher had just left for the US the night before, so he knew his secret was safe with him! After years of this kind of carry on I think he believed these stories himself.

As suggested earlier, the intermarriage of the ethnic groups which formed the population of Newfoundland produced a breed of independent individuals, and the village where I was born had its fair share of what today is known as *"characters"* but what we called *"queer hands"*. Usually, these odd individualists were possessed of a strong confidence in themselves, a fierce pride and often a wry sense of humour.

Howard Morry with his horse and slide
Morry Family Collection

At the time to which I refer, oil as a fuel for heating was unknown in the outports and only very few persons used coal on an occasional basis in their fireplace. Free for all purposes was wood which was cut in the nearby forests during the fall and winter, and a year's supply was brought out by horse and sled when the snow arrived.

For this purpose, each householder owned a small horse and this was considered a necessity by all. There were, however, some men who, usually because of lack of funds and land, did not own a horse. Such a man was a Calvert *"queer hand"*.

From time to time it was possible for men who did not own a horse to borrow one but, in the busy season, this was usually impossible. In such circumstances, those who did not own horses hauled their wood personally but were obliged to seek their fuel as near as possible to the village.

Like most men, our Calvert man was a fisherman, and like most fishermen, he built his own boat and maintained it. One year in a fall storm, his boat was badly damaged and extensive repairs, including installation of a new keel, were necessary. It was possible for him to get the majority of the timber required for the repairs in the nearby woods, but the keel was another matter. All trees large enough to produce a keel grew far from the village, and besides, it would be necessary to find a tree or two trees sufficient to produce the equivalent of two keels, one for himself, and the other for the sawmill in payment for sawing the wood. This arrangement, which was common during the Depression, was known as *"sawing on the halves"* - half to the owner of the wood, half to the owner of the sawmill.

When winter arrived, he set out to find appropriate timber for his repairs and quickly secured the necessary, except for the keel. For this, it was necessary to stay overnight in a hunter's cabin in the forest. It was also necessary to wait for late winter when the snow would melt a little by day and freeze during the night, allowing easy passage during the early morning. Finally, the time arrived and he left on his overnight journey hauling his sled, his axe and two days' food. He spent most of the first day reaching the forest area where he knew he would find spruce trees of the size required and where there was an old cabin to provide shelter during the night.

He then set forth in the late afternoon and, by dark, he spotted a number of trees which could possibly yield two pieces of timber such as he needed. He had already decided that it would be easier to have one very large log than two somewhat smaller ones. Early the next morning he was out again and by nine o'clock he had located a satisfactory tree, felled it and commenced to trim its branches. Before he finished this phase, the wind rose and snow began to fall, and he was forced to return to the cabin with the probability of spending another night with little food, though that did not disturb him. What did worry him was the certainty that the new snow would rot the old and he would no longer be able to travel over the top of the frozen snow, especially with a large log on his sled. This would mean much heavier going on the return journey.

All night the wind howled and the snow swirled around the cabin, but towards morning the sky cleared and our steadfast man made tea and finished the last of his food and prepared to leave. When he started outside, the worst of his fears were realised. When he trod on the snow, he sank to his waist and he knew that this condition would prevail for several days. His only alternative was to abandon the project until a later date or face a long hard haul. He decided on the latter. He quickly located his log, finished removing the branches and, with great difficulty, placed it on the sled and started his twelve-mile journey.

It is not necessary to describe the difficulties of this return journey, but it is easy to imagine the trials he faced during that day and most of the night while he covered the distance to his village. When he arrived home, he was spent and he was too tired to eat, although he had not eaten for nearly 24 hours, and only lightly at that time.

He slept for 12 hours, rested for a day and then decided to go to the sawmill, where he was greeted with astonishment and admiration when the details of his exploits became known. The owner of the mill agreed to saw "on the halves" and, in the absence of his son, who normally helped, the fisherman agreed to assist the mill-owner in the operation.

He was unfamiliar with the saw and when the log became immobilized momentarily as the saw met a knot in the wood, he pushed vigorously with his hand instead of using the pusher provided for such emergencies. In the process the saw severed his hand and he looked in dismay and terror at the dismembered hand and the flow of blood before he fainted.

In cases of emergency of this nature, the villagers always called both the Priest and the doctor. The former was usually more available than the latter, and also, he normally was the one selected to tell the family the bad news. When he came to, the Priest had arrived and crude first aid had been applied pending the doctor's arrival. The Priest was soon engaged in comforting John, saying it was God's will and *"God knows but it may be for the best"*. But, thinking of his labour to get the log to the mill and contemplating the life of a one-handed fisherman our man replied, *"Father, I know that you are doing your best to comfort me but you know what you are saying is dead wrong. God knows God damn well that it's not for the best!"*

Many other stories could be told about this *"queer hand"*, who may very well have been the real inventor of *"Spoonerisms"*. One time he came into Ferryland looking for the doctor to tend his wound and asked someone near the doctor's house on the hill, *"Is the doctor home?"* When he was told he was not, his response, without a thought of it being an odd thing to say was, *"Well if he's not home, he must be away."*! He is also credited with authoring the oft-heard opinion in Newfoundland that *"the worst thing a man could have on a house is no porch"*.

These are, however, representative anecdotes of a character who could be the sole subject of a book and in the broad picture I am painting, unfortunately, there is not enough space for more.

Another of the characters who richly deserves a mention is a man who lived on a hill in the centre of the village. He probably had some inner ear problem which caused some difficulty in balance. He was a shy man who, nevertheless, liked company and a drink of rum whenever he had sufficient funds available. He normally had difficulty walking a straight line but, when he had taken a few drinks, having this health condition, the results were impossible to forecast. Often when he was in this condition, the young boys would follow him, particularly if there had been recent rain, leaving puddles in the unpaved streets. We would watch as he took evasive action to avoid one puddle only to walk through a larger one, and his language was always colourful on these occasions.

He had been *"away"* to the mainland on two occasions, where he had worked on construction. One of his jobs there was in supply, and it was said he used to walk to the home of a friend 5 miles away and have the wife of his friend order the supplies because he was not familiar with the telephone and had no intention of becoming familiar with it.

Spreading salt fish to dry in Ferryland, ca 1935
*The man with the white hat at back believed to be Howard Morry
Morry Family Collection*

One day, he was shaving using a hand-mirror propped on the window while his mother was sweeping the floor. She asked him to move, and he did. He hooked his foot in a chair and fell out through the closed window into the vegetable patch in the garden. He was unhurt but the window-glass and vegetables were somewhat worse for wear and the air was purple with his language.

In the village, almost everyone went to Mass on Sunday morning. Sometimes in the winter, conditions would be hazardous because of sleet storms and frozen ice on the roads and it was necessary to proceed with great caution, particularly along the road by the ocean. In the early morning, when people rise in the outports, it is customary to step outdoors to view the sky and assess the weather, and often, in the case of men, to relieve their kidneys. One Sunday morning after a sleet storm, he did this, wearing his night attire, which for him was Long Johns. When he stepped outside, he slipped on the ice, slid across the narrow road near his residence, across an open field, across the main road by the sea, and only stopped when he reached the beach.

He now faced the task of getting back up the slope, which was very icy, in his bare feet, using one hand only, since he had to hold up his drawers with the other. He tried several times, only to slide back to the beach, and he now felt a sense of panic, for people were starting to go to Church and there was no place to hide. Soon there was a gallery of observers, alternatively shouting encouragement, suggestions and jokes, and, until some kid went for a rope, he continued to stand on the beach, one hand clutching his drawers, and the other raised aloft as he shouted oaths and obscenities. It is easy to guess the subject of the sermon at Mass that morning since the Priest was present during the latter part of the performance.

One day when his mother was serving his dinner, she dropped a large plate and broke it. He was momentarily angry with his mother and complained of her clumsiness. He rose to demonstrate how she could have avoided the chair which was in her way and had caused the crash. He tripped on the cat, fell on the open cupboard unit which contained the remainder of their dishes and brought it to the floor with a crash. When he finally looked at the mess there was one cup and saucer unbroken and he took these to the yard where he cut the wood, and broke them with the axe, saying to his mother, *"now we'll drink from the cover of the kettle."* He was a genuine character.

There was a woman in the village who was known for her meanness, and she had a small, quiet husband. He was illiterate, which was fairly common in those days since men went fishing as soon as they were able to escape from schooling. But whether he could read or write, he worked hard at the fishery and brought home whatever little he earned. He never spent any of the money he earned on himself; he gave it all to the wife. For her part, she didn't care if she got a meal or what it was and, a lot of the time, they ate out of tin cans. One day when he was talking to his friends down on the wharf waiting for the tide to turn, he said, *"You know the best 'mate'* [the way "meat" comes out in the local accent] *that ever came into this harbour is in that can with the dog on it."* And when his friends pressed him for further information it turned out that his wife had been feeding him dog food, unbeknownst to him.

In addition to the queer hands like those mentioned above, every village also seemed to have its own resident philosopher. Many of them were just local people who decided they would live in a bit of a different style and not be concerned with what other people thought of them. They were usually short on formal education, but long on the ability to think. Invariably, as in other pursuits, the village philosopher was not considered a success as a fisherman because he assigned a very low priority to success of any kind, and was only interested in gaining a modest livelihood. In my youth, my village had such a philosopher whom I have mentioned several times above.

He never owned a horse; he never owned much of anything, if it comes to that. His philosophy, as he told my father, was that *"the more you have, the more you have to worry about"*. In our family, we had horses, cows, sheep, goats and all kinds of fowl, and lots of property, meaning a lot of haying and odd jobs to be taken care of; he had none of this. He was a very endearing individual, a little leprechaun of a man whose moustache would stick straight out from both sides of his face whenever he got into an argument. And he was always looking for an argument on politics and every other topic of discussion that arose.

He was in many ways a brilliant man. He was logical and calm and was an original thinker. It was not uncommon for him to take a stance on an issue that was opposite to that of the majority of the villagers who, like the majority of men in general, placed a high value on material things and were affected in their thinking as a result.

He fished alone or with one of his sons when he did fish, and he also worked in the woods on the same basis. This was not because he was disliked by his fellows; on the contrary, he was well-liked, but he had no idea of time and was apt to be thinking of some abstract problem at a time when some practical act was necessary, and this often resulted in mishaps, which were, fortunately, generally of a minor nature. He would only go in the woods late in the day after being well rested up from staying up late the night before, and would not collect too much wood because he could see no purpose in having a lot of wood cluttering up his yard, even though this meant that the wood he burned would often be green and harder to light.

He was a happy man. His clothes were old and frequently second-hand, but since he wore them only for reasons of warmth and modesty, this was immaterial to him. He was supremely content if he had some tobacco for his pipe, a friend to have a good discussion, or better still an argument with, and, on occasion, a drink of rum or local moonshine.

I regret exceedingly that I was a grown man before I really appreciated the wisdom of this man and it was only then that I realized he had had a profound effect on me, although our discussions in my youth were few. While I spent many happy hours in his home playing cards with his wife and sons and other neighbours, I recall only a few discussions with him on relatively minor matters, but even so, I was impressed with his orderly thought processes.

Naturally, his tendency to ignore time and to do things without thinking, because his mind was otherwise occupied, sometimes had humorous consequences.

He wasn't handy at carpentry, or much of anything that required concentration, because his mind would always be on other matters. I recall once he built a fish-flake *[Editorial note: For those not from Newfoundland, this is a raised platform on which salt fish was spread to dry in the sun; seldom seen nowadays]* on the side of a hill below his house and *"stayed"* or anchored it by sinking long posts into the side of the hill and nailing them to the crossbeams of the flake. As anyone else would know, when you build on the side of a hill in that fashion, you need to put some of the stays downhill and leaning up against the flake to prevent the structure from slipping. He just concentrated on placing the uprights as vertical as possible so as to keep the platform of the flake level for walking on. When he and his son mounted the flake with a load of fish they'd just washed down by the ocean, the "stays" simply pulled free of the earth and the flake subsided with a *"whoosh"*. Fortunately, nobody was hurt, but he could not understand, no matter how much he thought about it, how this could have happened until the laws of physics and gravity were explained to him.

Once in a while, he worked for my grandfather (referred to as "old Tom" amongst my friends, to distinguish us) as a day labourer. This usually occurred when the fishery was in full swing and help was hard to find. My grandfather had two horses, the smaller, Bob, for ordinary chores and the other, Billy, for heavier work. One day he sent this man to get and make ready the smaller horse and, not hearing anything from him for some time, he went to look for him. Apparently, Bob had strayed away from him, and my grandfather found him in the barn looking in the hay-loft, and every conceivable place. When my grandfather asked, *"What are you doing?"* he replied *"Looking for the horse, sir."* My grandfather, a very stern man, often laughed about this afterwards, but at the time he was very angry; the horse might be small, but he was unlikely to be found in a barrel; he was agile, but he was unlikely to be found in a hay-loft!

Another time, my grandfather told him to *"tackle"* Billy, the larger horse, and take him for the haying in a neighbouring field, which was separated from the field where the horse was then situated by a four-rail fence. To reach the other field it was necessary to take the horse and mowing machine and go through a gate, down a lane and through another gate into the other field. After considerable time elapsed, my grandfather went in search and found him with the horse and cart still standing in the first field.

He shouted at him and said *"I thought I told you to take the horse and rig to the next field."*, to which our man replied, *"Will I take him through the gate, Mr. Tom?"*. *"No,"* said my grandfather, *"lift him over the fence."* The picture of this little man lifting a two-ton horse and rig over a four-rail fence was enough to send all present, including the man himself and my grandfather, into gales of laughter and was good for a laugh on many subsequent occasions.

I have spoken earlier of this man's total disregard of clothes from an esthetic viewpoint. Also, I have discussed how poor people were in the outports during the Depression. He had somehow bought or acquired one suit, which was intended for Sunday use only, and which was shared with his sons, except for the smallest one. He himself was only about 5 feet 5, his youngest son was about 5 feet 9 and the eldest was over 6 feet 1, and they were also different shapes, but the one suit had to do. On a Sunday, one of them would put on the suit and go to Mass and head home promptly. Then the next would put on the suit to go down to the usual men's Sunday gathering at the forge, an occasion one would not miss any more than Mass. Then that fella would go home and the last fella would get to wear the suit to evening prayers and for the rest of the evening. No one ever laughed at them because they were all that poor and they understood their predicament, but it was a comical thing to see these three wearing the same suit, more or less, depending on whether they could fit into it or not or it went beyond their hands and feet and the sleeves and legs had to be rolled up.

As I mentioned earlier, this man liked to smoke his pipe and, tobacco being expensive and money scarce, he never wasted any tobacco. When he put tobacco in his pipe, he made certain it was all consumed before he knocked the ashes from it and, even then, if he noticed any partially burnt particles, they were used with the next filling.

One Sunday morning, he arrived at the Church late as usual, and with his pipe going well. His routine was to wait until the priest passed his house in the car and then he would leave on foot. As he did not want to be too late, he looked at his pipe and, finding it still contained unburned tobacco, he put it in his pocket, held in his hand and entered the Church. The Priest had just commenced his sermon. Forgetting about the pipe, he removed his hand from his pocket to make the sign of the cross. Soon the parishioners began whispering and pointing at a veil of smoke arising from his pew, but he did not seem to notice anything. Finally, there was a shout and he came running down the aisle, both hands flailing at the front of his pants, while smoke billowed behind him. Once outside, he ran for a nearby brook and extinguished the blaze, but not before it had done considerable damage to his trousers, if not his dignity. One of the parishioners who went out to see if he was alright reported subsequently that he was lucky that he didn't completely destroy all his *"waterside premises"*.

All in all, he was a very Christian, God-fearing man who never, even inadvertently, used a word which could be considered vulgar. The *"F"* word, which is all too frequently heard today in mixed company, unfortunately, was a taboo in the days of my youth, and woe betide anyone who used it. The villagers had developed a whole set of other expressions to use which had the same force and were understood by all to be the same, even if they did not have the same shock value. One example of this is *"shag"*, which was the substitute for the other four-letter word referred to above.

He, knowing its real meaning, would not use this term. All was well until a new tobacco arrived on the market called *"Golden Shag"*. He liked this tobacco, but he could not or would not ask for it by that name. He finally developed a name which he could use, which would preserve his conscience and yet identify the product. To this day, the residents refer to this tobacco as *"Golden Sage"*, although the reason for that name is now known to few people.

Because he never had much money to spend, he would frequently run out of tobacco. But because he was well-liked in the village, someone would always help him out with a bowlful. One time, he went to St. John's and, with what little money he had, he bought the biggest pipe he could find. It would hold almost a quarter of a plug of tobacco. So, he began to carry two pipes with him. When my father offered him the full of his pipe, he would cut and cut and cut at the plug of tobacco and we were all watching him wondering what he was going to do with it all. Then he pulled this great bloody pipe out of his pocket and he filled it and tamped it down tight. And then he said to my father, *"If you don't mind, Howard, I'll save this to smoke after my dinner. Too precious to smoke it now"*. And he went off home. That night we were up at his house having a game of cards as usual and I saw him take all of the tobacco out of the huge pipe very carefully with his knife. And then he took out his little small pipe that you could scarcely get the top of your little finger into and he filled it and it hardly made a dent in the pile of tobacco he had taken out of the large pipe at all. He must have had about three days of tobacco because he was a very careful smoker.

I have referred earlier to the humour which is a part of life in the outports, even in adversity. Most of the villagers would not know the meaning of the word "pun" but they constantly employed that form of humour. They are also well-known for their ability to find humour in almost every situation.

It was customary for men to continue fishing into their 70's, and it was very difficult to persuade a fisherman to retire even when his family were well able to take care of his needs. I recall one such man, whom I will call Henry, who had a number of children, now adults, of whom some were unmarried. His children tried for years to persuade Henry to retire and he finally did in his 76th year. He did not take easily to retirement and was constantly telling the boys how to fish, and his daughter, who was his housekeeper, how to do her work, to a point where the family wished they had not persuaded him to retire.

Bill Morry and his father, Howard, spreading salt cod to dry
Photo by Dr. Stanley Truman Brooks, ca 1938
Provincial Archives Division, The Rooms

It was the practice in the village to allow all animals to live off the land during the summer, except of course for milking cows and the occasional horse which was needed. Every autumn, it was necessary to go in the woods and find the animals and bring them home for winter accommodation. The horses would be needed for the hay harvest and they would be brought back in August, but young heifers and bulls were allowed to roam until October or November, depending on the weather. Many families kept cows and young heifers as replacements for older animals and young bulls, which would be kept for a couple of years and then butchered for winter meat.

Martin Curran, ca 1935
Courtesy Steve Barnable (originally from Doug Furlong)

Henry's family had two cows, one of which was milking and kept at home, and the other a heifer, left to wander and feed itself, and each day, starting in August, being restless with nothing to do, Henry wanted to go fetch the heifer, but the boys continued persuading him to wait until October when they finally agreed that he should go and find the animal.

Henry set out at daybreak with his knapsack and kettle and the day passed until at dusk the boys began to worry about their father. About seven o'clock, as they sat in the kitchen discussing the possibility of raising a search party, they heard the gate open and their father's voice as he tried to get animal into the yard. His sons went to help and, in spite of the dark, they were able to drive the heifer into their field. The old man was fairly bubbling with enthusiasm regarding the growth of their heifer and he nagged one of his sons to take a look at how the heifer had *"growed"*. The son declined to go out because it was too dark to see but promised to do so in the morning. At the first sign of daylight, the old man called his sons but, since it was a windy day and they were unlikely to go fishing, they refused to get up.

Finally, one of the sons arose to please the old man and went with him to the nearby field. The old man again said, *"By Jeez, 'tis hard to believe how that heifer growed this summer"*. The son looked at the animal and then said, *"Yes, Da"*, *"and she growed an extra set of equipment too, that's Bill Sullivan's bull you got there"*. It was now easier for the old man to understand the reluctance of that particular animal to enter his property.

It was usual for *"old hands"* to go out each night before going to bed to look at the sky and forecast the weather of the next day. This visit also served the practical purpose of relieving themselves before retiring. During the late winter, in those days, it was important that that the snow froze so that it was possible to drive horses on top of the snow into areas otherwise very difficult to reach. The purpose of these forays was to cut and haul large timber for building and repairing boats, wharves, houses and other buildings. This period usually arrived after days began to be warmer, and it was necessary to have frosty nights following warm days to produce the best conditions. Some years, the right conditions do not occur and this was quite a setback to the fishermen.

One year the weather was very mild, and each night old Henry would go outside and observe the weather signs while he relieved himself. And each night when he came in, he complained about the *"softness"* of the weather, the term used locally for mild or warm weather. He couldn't wait for the cold and the snow to come so he could go into the woods and add to his woodpile, and that could not be done until not only the snow was there to slide on but the ponds were frozen solid. One night his son, having heard the old man say for perhaps the 20th time *"I've never seen it as soft afore"*, said, *"Geez, Da, what do you expect, you're nearly 80, it's time it got soft"*. While the old man did not appreciate the humour at first, he later told this story to all who would listen with a twinkle in his eye!

Another of old Henry's boys was contemplating the harvest and bragging of the yield and size of the crops. They were a family of hard workers and had a right to feel proud of what they grew. In those days, each family raised potatoes, cabbages, carrots and turnips in sufficient quantity for their annual needs, and these crops were kept in a special building called a cellar which consisted to a deep hole in the ground to prevent spoilage of the vegetables due to frost during the winter.

Before the potatoes were placed in the hole, it was necessary to ensure that they were completely dry and then place them in layers with a sprinkling of dry lime on each layer to ensure continued dryness.

One year, when Henry had his potatoes spread on the floor of the root cellar for drying, the weather outside being generally too damp to dry them outdoors, he noticed one morning that several of them had teeth marks on them.

Down below Henry's lived a family with several boys who were well known practical jokers. What Henry didn't know at the time was that these boys would have a hand in his problem with "rats".

Since it is not unusual for rats to do this, he obtained several rat traps and set them out in the evening. Next morning all the traps were sprung but no rats were caught, and several potatoes were again spoiled. he was complaining about this to anyone who would listen, so the neighbour boys got wind of it and decided to have some fun. For the next couple of nights, after Henry went to bed, they would sneak into his root cellar, set off all the rat traps and gnaw on a bunch of potatoes leaving teeth marks that could be mistaken for those of a rat.

This went on for several days and old Henry became more frantic and suggested sleeping in the root cellar but his sons vetoed this suggestion. At that point, he said, *"I must go down to M*$^r\cdot$ *Morry's store and get some rat bait and poison"* which my father carried in the store and supplied him with. But the next morning when he went out, he discovered the bait was all gone and the potatoes were again gnawed.

One morning, when Henry went to the cellar, he found the traps again sprung and the poison all taken without success, but instead of more potatoes with teeth marks, he found a sack with approximately the quantity of potatoes which had been spoiled. It was only then that it became clear that his problem was not with four-legged rats but with the two-legged practical joker *"rats"* amongst his neighbour's boys.

Old Henry lived well into his eighties and died quietly.
One of the local families had a number of children who had dropped out of school early, as was not uncommon in those days. Enforcement was negligible at best because, many times, the family needed all hands working to make ends meet. Yet, despite their lack of education, or perhaps even because of it, some of them displayed remarkable brilliance at times in their humorous responses to what might be considered obvious questions. There are numerous stories regarding this family, but only a few will be told to demonstrate this point.

The mother of this family had been dead for a number of years but, when one of the boys was visiting a nearby village, one of the residents there enquired, *"Is your mother dead yet?"*, to which the boy replied, *"Yes sir, she is dead yet"*.

The family, like most others of that time and place, was very poor, and it was not unusual for someone to wear boots or shoes with holes. The villagers repaired their boots and shoes themselves, but eventually, rubber boots, in particular, would wear beyond repair. Most of the male villagers wore rubber boots about all their working hours and it is necessary that they be *"waterproof"* or what is described locally as *"tight"*. In spite of their limited education, the boys in this family were all a witty bunch.

One day one of the boys of the family joined a group of boys at play while wearing a pair of boots with large holes. Now there is a streak of cruelty in many small boys and often too a need for *"one-upmanship"*, which caused one of the lads who could clearly see the poor condition to the boots to say, *"I see you got new boots on"*, to which he naively replied, *"They're not new boots, but they're new for me"*, since they were hand-me-downs. To this the smart aleck said, *"Are your boots tight."*, and he responded without missing a beat, *"Yes, they're tight. With six pairs of socks in them"*!

The family had a small coastal boat which they sailed to St. John's and into the villages along the coast, carrying freight when it was available. In those days there were very few trucks on the road between St. John's and the Southern Shore and few other ways to move freight. I once asked one of the boys, if he could steer the boat and he replied, *"Yes I can steer, but me brudder can steer faster"*, meaning his brother was a better helmsman than he was.

To eke out a living, they sometimes visited the French islands of St. Pierre and Miquelon, where they bought liquor at a low price for resale in Newfoundland. They also poached caribou and moose in areas where these animals were protected and sold the meat. The police eventually became aware of their various endeavours and began watching the ship as she traded along the coast.

One day, when she berthed at St. John's and the father was ashore trying to sell their contraband, the police boarded really only because the ship was docked where she shouldn't have been. One of the officers asked the son who was the only member of the family aboard where the captain was and the boy said: *"He's ashore sir"*. He then asked, *"Where's the mate?"*, to which the son quickly replied, *"We have no mate, sir, we only got bologna"*. Venison (caribou meat) at that time was out of season year-round. And, as we all surely know, bologna is about as far from meat as you can get! The police were too late on that occasion because truly there was no *"mate"*, it had already been off-loaded and sold.

During the Second World War, much construction was required in St. John's and, in the absence of so many men in the forces, labour was scarce and any men available were immediately hired if they were handy at all. The boys in the family I'm talking about were good workers and were soon working in construction at the new American base in town, Fort Pepperrell. Accommodations were hard to get but they found lodgings in a small boarding house down near Water St. where the food and lodgings left much to be desired.

The boys never had much and were easily satisfied, but the food served was so monotonous they were eventually driven to the point where they were ready to revolt. The daily diet, except for Sunday, consisted of porridge or one egg in the morning, boiled codfish and potatoes at noon, and beans, bread and tea, and occasionally a slice of bologna, in the evening; this menu never changed. Codfish was cheap at that time; you could buy them off the wharf for about ten cents each for a small one and about thirty-five cents would feed five or six men.

One day at noon, when one of the lads sat in the kitchen where they ate, he rose when the woman placed the inevitable boiled codfish on the table. She asked where he was going and he told her without smiling that *"We all loves codfish, ma'am; we eats it all the time at home; but if you keep feeding us codfish every day, we're all going to go down to the Waterford Bridge to spawn"*.

Eventually, the boys insisted on an improvement in the food and were adamant that they would leave if they did not get some meat. The landlady knew she had to do something or she'd lose a good thing, so she decided to buy some salt spare ribs to give the lodgers a "boiled dinner" on Saturday, as the boys used to go home on Sunday. She had rarely bought ribs for her own use and she was horrified at their price compared to the price of codfish, so she bought only three pounds, which was scarcely enough to flavour the vegetable water, considering that 2/3 of the weight is bone and salt, and the fact that she had four lodgers, herself and her husband to feed.

At that time Catholics had to abstain from meat on Friday, and that was part of the reason she decided to wait until Saturday to cook the ribs. That evening, when the beans were served and the lodgers continued their complaints, she told them what she proposed to have for dinner, not the next day, which was Friday, but on Saturday.

Saturday dinner time she placed the potatoes, cabbage, carrots and turnips on the plates (an insufficient quantity as usual) and with a flourish brought in the ribs on a platter and shared them in six portions. The meal was consumed silently and soon all plates were cleaned, yet nobody spoke. Finally, she said, *"Well boys, what did you think of the ribs?"* *"Well ma'am,"* one of them said, *"they were fine as far as they went, but I don't know why you had to wait until Saturday, you could have ate them on a Friday"*.

One man in Ferryland had lost his wife early on and found a lady friend in Cape Broyle, who helped him get over his grief. People got around on foot much more so then than now, mainly from necessity, as cars were scarce and horses were built more for pulling ploughs, not for riding. So, he would walk back and forth from Ferryland to Cape Broyle, a distance of more than 10 km, quite regularly.

It was his custom when visiting his lady friend to try and bring a little treat for her and, in those days, bakers' bread was considered a favoured treat, even though the home-made kind tasted better and was better for you. So, as he was heading up the road to Cape Broyle, he was carrying a loaf of bakers' bread with him in one hand and the other hand was shoved down in his pocket. One of my father's best friends met him on the road and said, *"Mornin' Sam, I see you have the staff of life in your hand."* *"Yes I do"*, the other man said, *"and I have a loaf of bread in the other one."*

My father told me a story about an incident that took place in the lead up to the Second World War when I was then living in the US. The news of the events in Europe heard over the few radios in Ferryland quickly spread by word of mouth to those who did not have such luxuries. One time, a terrible shrieking was heard in the main road ahead of the appearance of the woman who then assisted with nearly all births in the area at the time. She was running as fast as she could hollering at the top of her voice for everyone to leave town. The problem, it turned out, was that someone had heard the news that the Germans had taken Copenhagen and were killing all before them, and with her limited education, she mistook the geography and was shouting *"The Germans have landed at Cappahayden, the Germans have landed at Cappahayden, they'll soon be in Renews (about 20 km down the shore)."*

Jim Barnable (Centre) grading salt fish
Photo by Stanley Truman Brooks, ca 1938
Provincial Archives Division, The Rooms

Chapter 5: The "Boston States" in the Dirty Thirties

Editorial Notes:

My father's memoirs contained well over one hundred different anecdotes covering the time from his earliest remembrances until shortly after he moved us lock, stock and barrel to Ottawa after Confederation to take up a position of responsibility in the Canadian government. At first, I thought that I would cut off this book at the time of his first departure from Ferryland at the age of seventeen in 1937 to attend college in the United States. But then I realised that some of his anecdotes about characters, which I have included in the previous chapter, actually post-dated his departure by at least five years and were obviously "acquired knowledge" – stories passed to him by his father and others in the Ferryland either in letters to the States or in conversations beside the stove after his return to Newfoundland.

So, upon reflection, I decided that I really was justified in including at least some of the anecdotes in this and the final two chapters, which concern his time back in Newfoundland leading up to Confederation, and a brief glimpse at how his unique sense of humour carried over into his time as a "fed".

For those of you who are solely interested in memories of Ferryland, put down the book now; your reading is done. For the die-hards who have found something interesting, and hopefully humorous, about the way my father recorded his memories, I hope that you will bear with me and find these final chapters worth a read.

In regard to this chapter specifically, when my father graduated from high school in Ferryland, there was no university in which to pursue higher education then in Newfoundland. Memorial College was not a degree-granting institution at the time. An acquaintance of the family, Dr. Stanley Truman Brooks, an American zoologist from Pittsburgh who had stayed in the family home from time to time in the mid-1930s while conducting research on Newfoundland flora and fauna for the Carnegie Museum of Natural History, suggested that he travel to the US to study and agreed to sponsor him as a student immigrant.

By the time Dad reached the age of 16, he had already exceeded the capacity of the Newfoundland educational system to quench his boundless curiosity about the world. He had even taken correspondence courses in topics as arcane (to the Newfoundland school system of that time) as astronomy. So, the decision was made.

Although Dad did initially register for higher studies in electrical engineering at Pittsburgh Polytechnic, the bright lights of the US were too much for this naïve 17 year old to ignore and he spent his time in the US instead beating around in the seedier sections of South Boston, the Bronx and Brooklyn in New York City, Pittsburgh and other large cities working odd jobs to stay alive and learning how to box with the hope of one day competing in the Golden Gloves. He also became adept at playing poker and won enough to help support himself during a time when cash money was hard to come by in the States. In one game he won a diamond ring that was bequeathed to me when he died and which I recently passed on to his grandson, Peter, at his wedding in BC. He may have made the right decision to not pursue a diploma or a degree, for it certainly never hampered his career in later life. and it added great richness to the stories he could relay as a much-sought-after public speaker in future years.

Council of Higher Education
St. John's, Newfoundland
M. G. KING, SECRETARY

Sept. 24, 1937.

To whom it may concern:-

    This is to certify that the enclosed diplomas were awarded to Thomas G. Morry by the Council of Higher Education, the sole educational examining body in Newfoundland, and represent four years of High School work beginning with Grade VIII, together with two extra years at Grade XI, there being no facilities for the boy to go further at his home school.

    Grade XI is the equivalent of High School graduation in the U.S.A., and admits to the Memorial University College at St. John's, Newfoundland, as well as to the Canadian Universities, including those of McGill and Toronto.

    This pupil is eminently qualified to take up the work in a College in the U.S.A.

                          Faithfully submitted,

                                  Secretary.

Leaving school in Newfoundland for college in the USA, Sept. 1937
Morry Family Collection

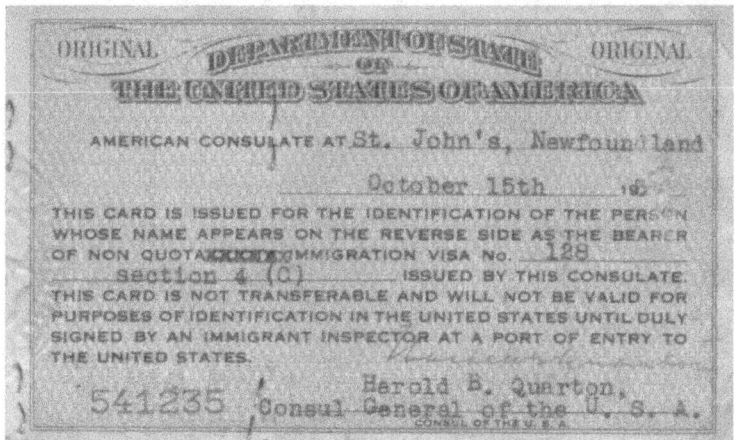

"Green Card" of Thomas Graham Morry, Oct. 15, 1937
Morry Family Collection

[Editorial note: Dad snuck back to Newfoundland and returned to the US again in 1938. But, as a landed immigrant, this was not allowed, so he falsified his green card by replacing the "37" with "38". Not a very professional forgery!]

When I was a young man I lived in South Boston for a while. Well, actually I was still a teenager at the time. Jobs were scarce in the Dirty Thirties in the US, and one would take any job offer. A man by the name of Maurice Devine, one of the so-called

"Remarkable Devine Family" from Kings Cove, Bonavista Bay, was by this time a successful contractor in Boston. *[Editorial note: A very real person, well-known to Newfoundlanders who, as my father says, always benefited from his love of fellow Newfoundlanders.]* He, in turn, hired a couple of his brothers and they together would hire any Newfoundlander who came along and who was looking for work.

 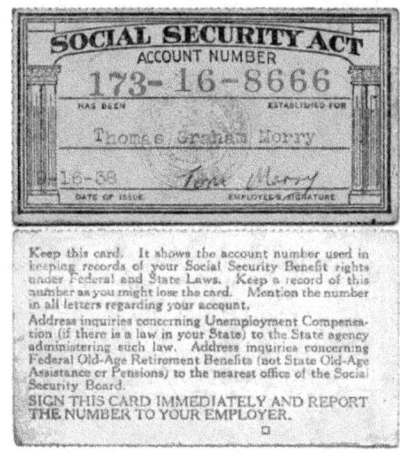

Thomas Graham Morry's Two Social Security Cards
Morry Family Collection

[Editorial note: Having left and re-entered the US between 1937-38 it was necessary to apply for a second Social Security Card to cover off detection of this illegal departure and re-entry. Note how he even disguised the handwriting of his signature on the second card.]

They hired me for a job at the Beacon Oil Company in New Jersey and one day, as we were painting the huge oil tanks for the company, which meant hanging on a rope seemingly high above the clouds, Maurice was observing and was dressed in his best white suit and Panama hat and white buck shoes; he always was a natty dresser. He didn't like the way one of the workers, Oley the Swede, was doing the job. He hollered up, *"Hey Oley, when are you going to learn to paint?"* Whereupon Oley, who had a bucket of red paint in his hand, turned it over onto Maurice's head from about twenty feet up. Well, you can imagine how angry Maurice was. He didn't know how he was going to get home to change. He couldn't get in the great big limousine he was driven around in because he would ruin the leather upholstery. So finally, the boys thought to wrap him up in a big tarpaulin and put him in the back seat of the car and the driver took him home.

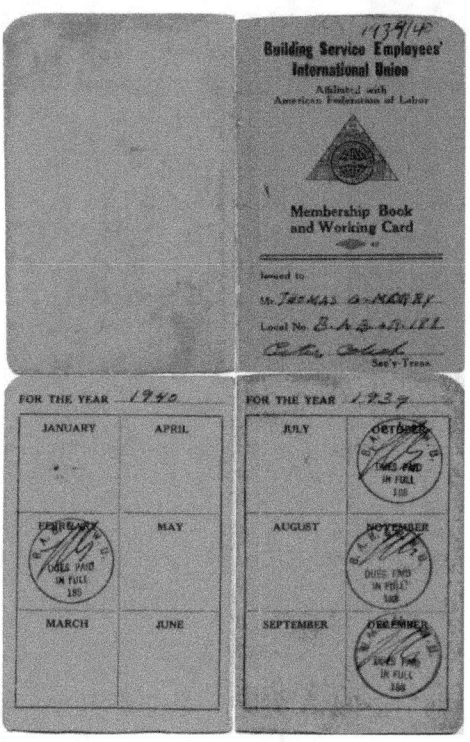

Dad's Building Service Employees' International Union Card
Morry Family Collection

He never fired Oley, though of course, he threatened to, and Oley offered to quit because in those days the bosses were mainly gangland members and he feared he might wind up dead. But Maurice wasn't one of them and, moreover, he had a pretty good sense of humour and saw that he had brought some of it on himself, no pun intended! So, he let it rest at that.

Billy Conn, "The Pittsburgh Kid"
Pittsburgh Boxing Facebook

When I lived in Pittsburgh, I was a member of the East Liberty Gym and I used to work out there with various budding boxers in the area. At the time I was there, Billy Conn, who afterwards became Light Heavyweight Champion, and fought for the Heavyweight crown, and Fritzie Zivik, a Middleweight contender, and I think Middleweight winner at one time, trained there, as well as Billy's brother, Jackie Conn, who wasn't much of a boxer and not much of anything else. In addition to these worthies, there were people like myself, merely a young fellow learning how to protect himself in what was a pretty rough town in those days. And also, the occasional beat up, worn out fighter who was past it but who liked to go into the gym to be among the up and comers of the boxing fraternity. One such person was a big tall black man who was called "Horizontal Hogan." I don't need to describe to you how he got that name!

T G Morry and fellow Newfoundlander, Ed Murphy
Photomat picture from Spear's Furniture Store, Pittsburgh, 1939
Morry Family Collection

Horizontal had two cauliflower ears and a flat nose, very few, if any teeth, and a permanent look of wonderment on his face. I guess he didn't know where he was half the time. He did, however, have some pretty damn good stories to tell. One of the stories he told me was that he was fighting an Italian from Brooklyn and the Italian was beating the hell out of him but his handlers kept telling him *"He's never laid a glove on you, you're doing alright, you're doing great. You're doing OK."* Then, he said, *"I'd go out again and he'd beat the hell out of me again and they'd drag me to the corner and freshen me up and tell me there wasn't a mark on me."* One time when he came in, however, his face was so misshapen, all gone to the left, he knew something had to be done and something had to be done fast. And he said to his handlers, *"What do I do, my face is all beat out on the one side."* So, his manager, Billy, said, *"You're letting him hit you too much with his right, block his right and let him hit you with his left and it'll straighten your face up!"*

Hogan, like a lot of other people when they get older, got religion, and, at that time, the charlatan evangelist Father Divine *[Editorial note: A real person but obviously no relation to the Maurice Devine mentioned earlier.]* was operating his big estate on the Hudson. He was one of those early evangelists who used to encourage people to come and live on his estate and, according to how much money they gave him, he would make them an angel or an archangel, or merely a worker. Well anyway, old Hogan saved up whatever few cents he had left and he went down to Father Divine and Divine said, yes, he would take him in, he was a worthy case, but he could only be one of the people who worked and helped with the collections in the church, and so on. He said that the Father would have a habit at the end of his service of telling how much he needed money and he would tell the congregation, *"Dig, dig deep, and give it all."*

Hogan said one day they were taking up the collection and there was not as much money in it as Father Divine thought that there should be. He didn't want to accuse the collectors, as it was pretty hard to get people to do that; it was a job most people don't like. And besides, how do you make sure that they are honest anyway? So, he devised a scheme that worked. In the words of Hogan, *"The Father knew what to do. He put a boxing glove on my right hand and told me to take up the collection with my left hand."* All the other collectors, boxers or no, were required to follow suit. He said the collections went up dramatically after that.

Chapter 6: The War Years and Confederation

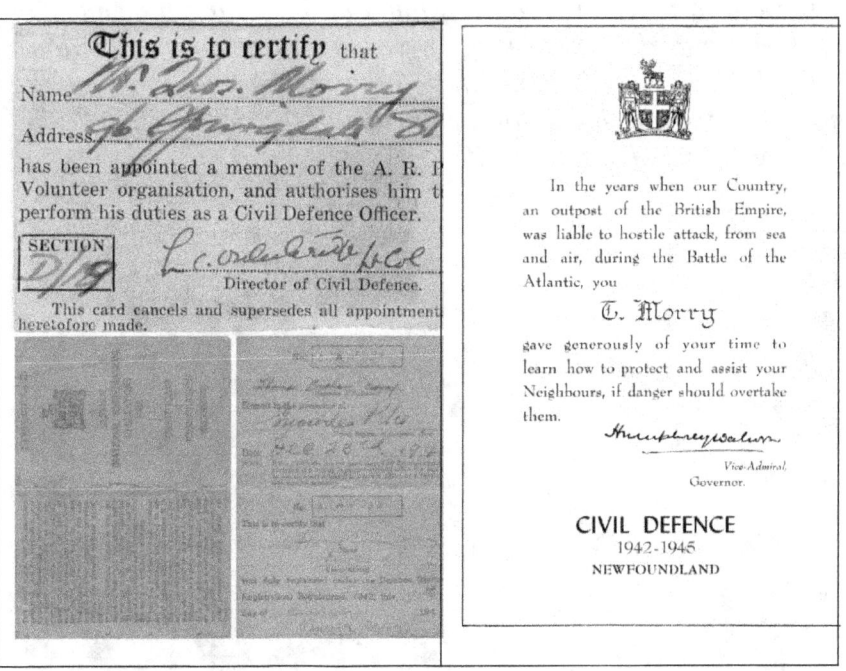

*T G Morry's Air Raid Precaution Volunteer and
National Defence Registration Cards and Certificate of Service
Morry Family Collection*

Editor's Notes:

Dad may have chosen to stay in the US and build a life for himself but for the outbreak of WWII. When he learned that his younger brother, Reg, had already joined the Royal Navy even before war was declared and that his older brother, Bill, was now with the Newfoundlanders in the Royal Artillery, he wanted in on the action and headed home to Newfoundland. However, when he got there, he learned that the Newfoundland government, having learned from sad experience in WWI the cost of allowing too many sons from one family to join the forces, no longer allowed a single family to contribute more than two sons to serve at a time. Instead, he wound up becoming a member of the home guard and working in various government positions. This chapter and the one that follows describe some of the incidents, real or imaginary, that we are told occurred during this interesting phase of his life.

Brothers Bill (Royal Artillery) and Reg (Royal Navy) ca 1939
Morry Family Collection

Dad never did return to Ferryland really, except on visits. When war broke out and he returned to Newfoundland he stayed in St. John's and found work easily enough in the government. Many men were of course overseas, leaving vacancies that were filled by women as much as possible – the first time in Newfoundland history when women were even considered for "men's work". In fact, during these years, his future bride, Evelyn Wheeler, rose to a position as close to the top in the Revenue Department as the still narrow-minded employment officers would permit.

But even with women filling the ranks, many vacancies still existed, so finding work was no problem for a bright, able-bodied young man.

I hope that some of his adventures recounted below will resonate with some "townies" who have no doubt felt left out of the discussion up to this point.

In the early days of my career, I used to work in City Hall in St. John's as an auditor for the Commission of Government when the government was giving the city grants for operations which we had to audit. There were a great group of characters around there at the time, both in the office and also as elected representatives on the Council.

The mayor of St. John's for ten years in the late thirties and early forties was a man named Carnell, who also ran a funeral parlour.

[Editorial note: There is no point trying to disguise this person with a pseudonym. He was too well known and stories like these are common.]

I never saw a man who looked more like a mayor than Andy Carnell. He was a self-made man, fairly wealthy, but a man who never moved far from his humble beginnings as far as his speech was concerned and his reactions to things around him. He was, in fact, a strange kind of man. But everybody knew him well, personally or by the reputation that preceded him: *"Andy was a Dandy"*, they said. He used to wear the finest suits, with a waistcoat and a big gold chain across and a pince-nez, he had silver-grey hair which was always meticulously trimmed and combed.

T. G. Morry, Centre Back, Friends and Workmates, Topsail, 1941
Morry Family Collection

Andy used to drink a fair bit during the day. He'd send out the doorman, whom we called the rum runner, to get him a couple of bottles and he drank moderately but continually all day so that he was never unable to perform his duties. He could have remained mayor for the rest of his life if he had wanted to because any man that met him in the street who asked if he'd like to share a drink, he'd go along with no matter what else was happening.

He would take all the phone calls coming in - no screening. One day, after about three days of rain, he got calls from everyone about flooded basements and he was beginning to get browned off about this. Especially when he got a call from a woman from the South Side. She said, *"Is that mayor Carnell."* *"Oh yes,"* He said, *"this is your Mayor."* He tended to put on a very affected kind of tone when he answered the phone. *"Yes, what is your* trouble, madam?" She said, "My basement is flooded." "Oh, that's too bad, where do you live, we'll try to help you if the water is coming from the common property onto yours." Then we heard "You want to make a claim for what? You say your hens drowned? Dammit woman why don't you keep ducks; you know the South Side always floods down off the hill in the rain" and he banged down the phone.

Another time I was listening to the one side of the conversation when he picked up the phone and it went something like this: "Oh, yes this is he, this is your mayor, Mayor Andy Carnell...yes...yes...yes...no...no...no, by the Lord suffering Jazuz!" and he hung up the phone.

Andrew Greene Carnell (1932-1949)

From Memorial University Website

Because he was the mayor, Andy was invited to every event that was worth a damn, and this was particularly so for weddings. And he had the proper clothes for all occasions. He would be turned out during the day in Morning Clothes for some kind of reception and in the evening in full tails with top hat and all, always the proper dress for the occasion. Andy was always the same, he would nearly always drink more than he should and he would nearly always make a spectacle of himself afterwards. One day I was going into the Newfoundland Hotel to go up to the Burns Dinner that was going on and, as I walked up to the large marble steps in the lobby, I met a man's behind in a pair of striped pants, coming down the stairs backwards on his knees. This was Andy backing down over the stairs on his hands and knees so that he wouldn't fall over the stairs, he was that high! He knew once he made it to the front door that someone would call him a taxi to get him home because everybody knew him and everybody liked him. Or nearly everyone!

One of the representatives on City Council during the time that Andy Carnell was Mayor was a man called Jimmy Spratt.

[Editorial note: Another real person whose identity and behaviour are a matter of public record and hence impossible to hide.]

Jimmy was a retired contractor. The two of them were bitter enemies. They fought over everything; whatever one said, the other said the opposite. It would usually end up in a shouting match at the end of the Council meetings. I remember one day sitting in the office and hearing a great outcry out in the hall. One of my coworkers, Ray Haley, and I went out to see what the trouble was. The Mayor was coming down the stairs as fast as he could go with his pince-nez hanging on the chain bouncing up and down, and chasing him with his coat off, and taking off his vest, which he always wore, even on the hottest day, was Jimmy Spratt, and he hollering at the top of his voice, with all the taxpayers in the office and everything else, *"You!"* he said, *"You, the Mayor of St. John's? You're not fit to be the Mayor of an outhouse!"* Only he used a more colourful word for such a structure.

Another day, Jimmy brought in a bundle of flowers to give to one of the so-called "girls" who worked in the office, though none of them had been girls for thirty years or more. She was a woman well advanced in years, almost ready for retirement. And Jimmy used to make a big play for her every day he came in. He'd sweep off his derby hat and bow from the waist. He was like a damn Irish leprechaun! He had a big moustache and twinkling eyes; a dandy little Irishman who would fight at the drop of a hat. But he seemed to have a real case on this woman. And this day he arrived with a great big bunch of long-stem roses. Even she seemed to be impressed, she didn't say *"Go on, you old fool"* when he proffered the roses to her and bowed deeply from the waist.

And after he had done this and he saw that she had not completely shut him off, he bent down and he whispered in her ear and you can conjecture what he said. Because she said, *"Get out of here you dirty, foul-mouthed brute!"* So, he was taken aback, because all the Councillors were looking, and all the people at the counter paying their taxes were all looking in. So, he took the big bundle of roses he had just brought in, I don't know how much he had paid for them but it didn't matter, and he took them by the stems and he started beating her around the head with the roses and the petals flying everywhere and leaves flying everywhere. The people at the next desk were ducking the fragments that were flying around.

Haley and I had to take him out and cajole him into leaving the room, but he was still going right off of his head, he couldn't believe that she had given him that short answer to his *"sincere"* proposition!

As I said, Jim had been a contractor before he became a City Councillor, and he had also been a Member of the House of Assembly under the old government and worked for the Commission of Government after that, and wound up being a Minister of the Crown after Confederation. But one time he told me he was taking part in a filibuster in the House of Assembly to try and talk down a bill presented by the government of the day that was not supported by his party. So, he was going on at great length about all the lighthouses he had built when he was a contractor. Someone on the other side of the house shouted across, *"You built a lot of lighthouses, Jim?"* *"Yes,"* he said. Then the voice said, *"Did you get paid for them?"*, Jim didn't see it coming so he said, *"Yes, I did."* Then the voice said, *"Well then shut up and sit down."* He was so taken aback that he did indeed sit down and thereby lost his chance to filibuster and the next speaker took the floor. The Speaker wouldn't let him get up again and they lost the vote on the bill.

At this time, there were a couple of collectors at the city who would go out to collect unpaid taxes, for which they received a small salary and a percentage of what they were able to collect. One of them was a very straight-laced Presbyterian who rarely if ever took a drink or said anything out of the way. And the other was a little devil-skin who was always drunk, who shall remain nameless. They threatened to fire him several times but no one was fired very easily at City Hall because if they were going to fire them for drinking there would have been nothing but a few of the girls in the whole place - everybody drank there during working hours.

But anyway, finally they were so browned off with him that the Chief Clerk called him in and said: *"I don't want to fire you but I will give you one last chance. If you don't sign the pledge and give up this drinking, I'm going to have to discharge you."* He said, *"I'm serious this time. I cannot impress upon you enough that I am not going to give you another chance after this."* This man used to take some of the back taxes he collected and buy a bottle of rum and go up on Signal Hill and drink it. It wasn't that he was dishonest, as he would always pay it back, but it was just too much of a temptation when he had no money of his own, which was much of the time. Anyway, we were all at the office at the time that the collectors normally came back and we were wondering if he would come back and, if he did, would he be drunk.

About a quarter to five (we closed at five o'clock) this apparition came in, staggered across the hall, waving a piece of paper above his head and looking towards the main office of the City Clerk. He headed for the door. We tried to stop him because it was clear he was loaded drunk. But he wasn't to be deterred. He was waving his arms around his head and he said, *"Mr. Mahoney, I signed the pledge, I'm not going to drink anymore."* The City Clerk opened the door and the collector fell in on the floor. He said, "Why, you are drunk. And you signed the pledge?" To which he responded, *"Well I had to have one to celebrate."*

As I said, most of the people who worked for the city used to drink on the job. There was one fellow in there who used to drink as much as anyone else but he reformed and quit drinking. But before that, he was something else. He would do anything; he didn't know what he was doing sometimes. He hated his job, he hated the City, he hated the Mayor and he hated the City Clerk, all with equal intensity. So, one day he was on a drunk and Ray Haley and myself were at Dennie Fong's, which was the Chinese place next door where we used to go now and again to have a drink and a laugh.

Well, this man reeled by the place and he was drunk. He had a Derby hat on, they all wore Derby hats, and it was turned down over one eye, and you could tell that he was pretty high, the very look of him, the way he was navigating. So, Ray and I followed him into the office. His coat was hanging by the door and the hat was on it, but no sign of him. But the door to the big iron vault where the records were stored was open and, in the vault, we could see him but we couldn't see what he was doing. As we snuck over to the vault to see what he was doing, here he was with his fly open relieving himself up and down on the ledgers that were stacked on the other side of the vault, and he had a big foolish grin on his face, and laughing as he did. Now one thing was, he could have gone to the washroom, but I guess he was raring to go and he wanted to go, and he felt this would be a good thing to do anyway. So, he was enjoying himself, but Haley and I used to handle those ledgers with care for some time afterwards!

One of the principal forms of entertainment in Newfoundland was the frequent elections, which nevertheless, in the mind of many people, did not occur frequently enough. Particularly in the outports where other forms of entertainment were scarce. I used to go home to Ferryland to vote and to take in the associated *"entertainment"*.

The villagers flocked to the parish hall for the political meetings and there was no lack of repartee between the speaker and the audience. Usually, the meeting ended peacefully enough, but occasionally when the speaker was personally unacceptable, or had unacceptable proposals, or represented a party, not in favour, there was no assurance that peace would prevail.

On one occasion during a particularly bitter campaign, the candidate who represented the party in power was unwelcome, and this became apparent early in the meeting. He persisted, however, and the word was passed around *"sod him"*, the Newfoundland version of tarring and feathering. He may have noticed people leaving the hall, but neither this nor their return had any significance for him until he was hit by the first wet sod torn from the embankment near the hall.

By the time the flight of sods finished and the candidate's flight began some rake said that it was necessary to use a bulldozer to find him. There were variations of this unique way of expressing strong disapproval of course. On one occasion, three-day-old squids were used, and anyone who has smelled rotten squids does not need any further description. To those who have not savoured the ambiance, it is sufficient to say that, compared with the rotten squid – or rather hundreds of them – a skunk is like an expensive French perfume.

A cousin of mine in St. John's was married to a lawyer whose name was Rex Renouf.

[Editorial note: Again, this is his real name, but since he was married to a relative and was very well known it cannot be disguised.]

He was a very thin man, quiet and reserved. Everybody wondered why he went into politics, as it did not seem like him, but he did. So, he was going around attending the usual rallies before the election. He arrived in Ferryland for a meeting in the village hall and was getting ready to make his speech and was sitting on the stage, quite evidently nervous and looking more dead than alive. His wife, Peggy, was sitting down in the audience alongside a Ferryland fisherman. And he was observing her applause whenever her husband took part in anything, so he deduced that this was her husband, but he wanted to find out. So, he leaned over and said to her, *"Hey missus, is that your husband up there?"*. *"Yes,"* she said proudly *"that's him"*. *"My God!"*, he said, *"Shockin' t'in ain't he?"*

There were very few opportunities for patronage in those days of economic distress, but those which existed were used to full advantage; maintenance jobs on the highway, if it could be called a highway, and on the railway, as well as post office operator and contracts to deliver the mail were bestowed to supporters of the party in power and removed as rapidly with each change of government. "Fence-straddling" during elections by those holding these jobs was completely unacceptable. Each job-holder was forced by his fellow residents, the candidates or his workers to declare himself publicly. He could vote as he wished but his public declaration was the only factor considered when it came time to review the patronage slate.

It was not unusual for members of the same family to adopt strongly partisan but divergent political attitudes to keep the job in the family and sometimes it worked. This required considerable acting ability, for it was necessary to support the declared political stands with public disagreements and sometimes quarrels. One family, by the use of such tactics, was successful in keeping the road maintenance job in the family for many years in spite of the best efforts of other applicants. I once asked an old partisan what it was like to be a political partisan or a politician during the period referred to. He answered by asking me if I was aware of how trees could be aged by the rings of growth and then told me that there are rings of fat and rings of lean meat on his body depending on when his political party was in power.

It is indeed strange that those who decried the system I have described were often the strongest supporters of a return to more of the same when Britain decided to terminate Commission of Government in 1947.

The elections were often pretty messy and dicey affairs, with dirty tricks being more blatant, though not necessarily more common, than they are today. Free rum was an essential tool of all parties going on the hustings. Religion played a much more prominent role in elections in those days in Newfoundland, as it had done since the commencement of Responsible Government in 1855.

There is an old story that was going around about an even before my time that is worth retelling. In one riding, Holyrood, Conception Bay, the chances of anyone other than a Roman Catholic winning was very low, in fact virtually non-existent. Sir John Crosbie was leading the United Newfoundland (i.e. Conservative) party at the time (1928-1932).

He himself was running in a nearby riding (Brigus) and he needed the whole district to be able to hold onto power. He looked like he might be winning over the people out there even though he was a Protestant. Leading up to an election, the parties or their supporters used to print little "newspapers", really nothing more than partisan propaganda, and spread them around the district liberally in hopes of persuading the voters on the fence with what would today be called "false news". Other forms of communication were virtually non-existent at the time. Radio did exist, but almost no one owned a receiver.

On the night before the election, long after the law said there should not be any further politicking, one of the old freight trains was going out across the country and, when it reached Holyrood, they dumped off three or four bundles of papers, which were ostensibly the "official" voice of Sir John's party. Right away a bunch of people moved in and distributed these far and wide throughout the riding. Next morning, when people went out on their doorstep, here was the paper masquerading as the voice of the United Newfoundland party with the headline reading: "Sir John Crosbie says the Pope can kiss my ass!". The Liberal party took the riding and the election. True or not, it makes a good story!

There was another story going around that I cannot personally vouch for but that is worth the retelling.

In the outports, before the days of television, when even radios were rare, not only the elections, but any event was a diversion and full advantage was taken of it. The annual garden party was, of course, the première occasion of the year. The arrival of the train or the coastal boat in the more remote communities was enough to cause all those available to gather. But the coming of the Circuit Court was one of the prime diversions of spring and fall.

On one occasion, the Magistrate who was travelling with the Court was a pious and somewhat sanctimonious person who demonstrated in his manner to all and sundry that he was above the human frailties of the common herd and that he knew this to be so. He always dressed carefully in dark clothes with a hard bowler hat, yellow gloves, white spats and a white scarf and always carried a cane. He was precise in his manner and speech to the point of fetish and never used a word that could be construed to be offensive to anybody. He was the kind of man who would never use one word where he could use ten.

Court was held in the parish hall, and all the residents of the village, young and old, big and small, who could get there were present when the Magistrate arrived. He was somewhat surprised by the attendance but was quite happy, as it would be a good occasion to be at his "pedantic best" and to demonstrate his superiority to the local residents.

The first cases were routine, an argument over ownership of a boat, a boundary dispute and simple theft, and then the clerk called the case against one of the local young men accused of being the father of a child of a local girl who was well-known as being of easy virtue. She was suing for support of her child, or at least her parents were, and the problem was to establish paternity. This is what they did in those days, the man would get hauled into court so he'd have to provide some measure of support in any case. So, she had named this man as the father and he was subsequently summoned to appear before the court.

For this particular Magistrate to be hearing a case of this sort in an outport in Newfoundland was somewhat of a travesty because no one could understand a word he was saying. The Magistrate sat on the platform, very ill at ease, as the young man was called to the stand and entered a plea of not guilty, and the Magistrate became visibly more disturbed after the plea for he would now have to establish the facts of the case, as neither of the parties was represented by a lawyer, as is generally the case.

As *"Mary"* was called to the stand, the stillness of the Court was broken by whispers, some quiet laughter and the opening and closing of the entrance door as some prudent men left the room in case they might be implicated in her testimony. The Magistrate haughtily called for order and Mary was sworn, after which he began to question her. Mary was hard of hearing, so the Magistrate, who started questioning her in a low voice, was obliged to raise his voice almost to a shout.

Magistrate: *"Why are you here, Mary?"*
Mary: *"Because he knocked me up, Yer Honour."*
Magistrate: Pretending that he did not understand the term, *"He did what?"*
Mary: *"He knocked me up."*
Magistrate: *"Tell the Court what happened."*
Mary: *"Well Yer Honour, I was walking over the barrens to Cape Broyle along with my boy, Jim, when I met Jack, who was going in the other direction. We stopped to talk and he asked me if I would go in the woods with him…"*
Magistrate: *"Did you go?"*
Mary: *"Not right away, you see I had my boy with me and…"*
Magistrate: *"How old is the boy?"*
Mary: *"Seven years, Yer Honour."*
Magistrate: *"Proceed."*
Mary: With hand behind ear, *"Whaa?"*
Magistrate: In loud voice, *"Go on with your story."*
Mary: *"Well he started pushing me off the road and put his arms around me."*
Magistrate: *"What did you do then?"*
Mary: *"I told him we'd have to do something with Jim."*
Magistrate: *"What did he do?"*
Mary: *"He took off his necktie and tied Jim to a tree."*

By this time, the amusement of the audience was interfering with the interrogation and the Magistrate was forced to call for order and threatened to clear the Court. He then resumed the questioning.

Magistrate: Fearfully, *"What happened then?"*
Mary: *"He took me into the woods and laid me down."*
Magistrate: *"On the ground?"*
Mary: *"Yes, Yer Honour, but he put some boughs under me a**e."*
Magistrate: *"Clerk, do not enter that word in the record --- under your rear, Mary?"*
Voice from the crowd: *"There is nothing rare about what Mary has."*
Magistrate: Amid loud laughter, *"Order in the Court; continue Mary."*
Mary: *"Then he pulled up my clothes, got between my legs and started doing it."*
Magistrate: *"Only once?"*
Mary: *"No, no Yer Honour, he did it twice."*
Magistrate: *"Did he remove your underwear?"*
Mary: *"I don't wear no drawers, Yer Honour."*
Voice from audience: *"She's always ready for action."*
Magistrate: *"Order!" "Did you copulate?"*
Mary: With hand behind ear, *"Whaa?"*
Magistrate: *"Was there penetration?"*
Mary: *"Whaa?"*
Magistrate: *"Did you have sexual relations?"*
Mary: *"Whaa?"*
Magistrate: *"Were you as man and wife?"*
Mary: *"Whaa?"*
Magistrate: *"Did you consummate the act?"*
Mary: *"Whaa?"*
Magistrate: By now at his wit's end and obviously disturbed, *"This girl does not understand simple English."*

Magistrate: *"Look around you now. I want to ask you who you had sexual relations with. Look carefully. Did you have sexual relations with that man in the dock there?"*
Mary: *"No, Yer Honour."*

The Magistrate was quite put out now and not knowing what to do. But Mary piped up: *"But I did it with him, and him, and him"* indicating several others, as the court rapidly cleared with the guilty parties falling over one another to get out of there.

Among the interesting characters in Newfoundland in more recent times was a man by the name of Billy Browne.

[Editorial note: His real name; but once again, impossible to disguise considering the positions he occupied.]

He reached the level of being a Supreme Court Judge in Newfoundland and he once sat in the Diefenbaker Cabinet in Ottawa as Solicitor General. Billy was a religious fanatic. He felt that everything revolved around and could be settled by prayer, which would be alright if he felt that way and kept it to himself, but he tended to impose his judgements on others. This could lead to some very interesting situations.

For many years, there was a train running out of St. John's on the 24th of May weekend called the *"Trouters Special"*. It would stop at every pond where someone wanted to get off and pick up all hands on the way back a day or so later. And that train was usually an unorganized drunk; by the time it was an hour out of St. John's, everyone was higher than a kite, singing and telling yarns and so on. And in one of the particularly rowdy cars all was going well when Billy Browne came in and called for silence. And when he got some modicum of silence he said: *"I want two more hands to say the rosary."* Well, you can imagine what happened – the noise, the oaths, throwing bottles and everything else. He was lucky to escape with his life!

Another time Billy Browne was on the bench and he had a fella before him by the name of Michael Patrick O'Brien.

[Editorial note: Possibly a real name, but it is so common it hardly matters!]

He was charged with having broken into a store and stolen some goods. And it wasn't his first offence. Billy, looking at his name, was very surprised; surely a good Catholic boy like him couldn't be involved in a crime of this sort. So, inspiration struck him and he started asking questions. First, he asked:
"Michael Patrick, do you say your prayers every day?"
"Yes, Your Honour, I do."
"Do your parents say their prayers?"
"I think they do, Your Honour."
"Do your parents go to church?"
"Yes, they do, Your Honour."
"Do you go to church?"
"Yes, Your Honour."
By this time, Billy was more confused than ever. He couldn't figure out the pattern at all. Suddenly another inspiration struck him and he said:
"Tell me, Michael Patrick, did you make the mission?"

There had just been a mission at the Roman Catholic Cathedral.
"No, Your Honour."

So, Billy said to himself *"Aha!"* He said:
"Why didn't you, Michael Patrick?"
"Because I go to Wesley Church, Your Honour."
"Thirty Days", said Billy.

Another time, two ladies of the night came up before Billy accused of being streetwalkers. They had been at the game for quite a while; in fact, they were up before this Magistrate for the same charge for perhaps the tenth time. So, Billy decided that he was going to try and save them, especially since their names were Murphy and O'Connell. The Magistrate was also of Irish ancestry and very proud of the fact. He was also religious to the point where he outdid the Priests and Monks. On this occasion, the facts were quickly related by a Police Officer in modest language, which they had all learned to use when appearing before this particular Magistrate and the women pleaded guilty.

The Magistrate, before passing sentence, addressed the accused and said, *"Aren't you two ashamed of yourselves? Here you are with two fine Hibernian names and yet you are guilty of this moral degradation, can't you give up this way of life. At least can't you give it up during the holy season of Lent?"*

There was always a chance of this kind of scene when that particular Magistrate was on the bench and his Court was always crowded. He had his own explanation for this and he was heard telling friends that it was because his wisdom and intuitive Judgement were of such a high order.

During WWII, when the bases were being built in St. John's, workers would flock in from the outports for the cash income in the building trades, something that was still uncommon in the barter and trade of the fishery. Of course, the rude skills developed in building houses, boats and wharves around the bay were more than adequate in that context but were less than what city building contractors were used to in town, and some of them were pretty arrogant in their disdain for the workmanship of the outport men.

When the Americans were hiring in Newfoundland to build their bases in Goose Bay, Labrador and in Stephenville, Argentia and Pleasantville (St. John's) on the island, they had some odd requirements of the applicants. For example, they used to insist that a man have a good set of teeth, presumably to be sure that they would be able to get by on rough food until they got their kitchens established. I mentioned earlier that in Newfoundland many men, by the time they were in their twenties, had already lost their teeth due to bad hygiene and worse nutrition and that they often wore off-the-shelf false teeth which were locally called "China Clippers."

There was a great gathering of people in front of the building where the interviews were taking place wanting to be hired because these were solid jobs with good pay, and that was hard to find at the time. Word went around that there was no point going in there if your eyesight wasn't good, if you were infirm in any way, or if your teeth were not sound. They would, however, accept a man with dentures. One poor fellow wanted a job in the worst kind of way, but he had neither tooth in his head and he didn't own a set of China Clippers. So, he was desperate to figure a way out of it. He told his friend who was with him, who did have a set of China Clippers, to go in first. Shortly he came back, delighted with himself because he had been hired. So, the other fella said, *"Norman, give me your set of teeth"*, not an ordinary request by any means, and not something you would want to do too often, but he did, and his friend got a job too.

During my apprentice days in accounting, I used to work for a man called Nimshi Crewe, to whom I owe very much for my training in accounting.

[Editorial note: His real name. I thought of replacing it with an alias, but he was quite well known, and it would be a thin disguise at best.]

Nimshi was a genius but he was also more than likely an undiagnosed schizophrenic. Every now and then the poor man would check himself in at the Waterford for shock treatment, the first time I'd ever heard about shock treatment. He'd go in and he'd come out and he'd be all right for a while and go on, and eventually, he would build up to the same condition again. He was a man with a magnificent mind. He probably didn't have anything more than high school education, in fact, I'm sure he didn't. But he was a mathematical genius; he could add up a row of figures six wide in his mind and then say, *"now check that out Morry"*, and I would do so with an adding machine and his total was always correct.

He was a great accountant. He knew all about balance sheets and all the other paraphernalia of the accounting trade. He was also a great debater and was always in high demand at the MCLI, which was the Methodist College Literary Institute, as a debater against renowned people with great educations. He could always more than hold his own. More on this in a moment.

But despite all that, he was a bit of an oddball. Not that it would stand out today, but at a time when nobody wore a beard, he wore a beard.

I remember one day getting on a bus at the auditing office going down to the other end of town. And down at the back of the bus there was a loud singing of *"Let Jesus Be Your Guide"* and I looked down and there was a well-known local drunk about the town, a hard-working man but a drunk nevertheless, and an irreverent guy, and joining him in song this day was the Deputy Auditor General, Nimshi Crewe! And a woman said to me *"Isn't it scandalous, those two drunken men down there singing."* And I said *"Ma'am the man with the beard is not drunk"*, though apparently, he must have staggered when he got in. When we got off at the station, he gave me a lecture on decorum because of some little contretemps I had with someone working for the railway. He was a great one to speak of decorum!

Offer of Employment from Nimshi Crewe to Thomas G. Morry, 16 July 1940
Morry Family Collection

Another time we were auditing a savings bank and he had kept us working overtime because he had a deadline on getting the job done. He used to do his own typing; he'd stop in the middle of the job and run over to get on the typewriter. There were big long metal benches in the bank and the metal typewriter was on the bench. So, while Nimshi was occupied elsewhere, one of the auditors, who was never up to much good, always boozing, ran a wire from the typewriter and stuck the end in the socket that was on the bench. Nimshi came back, there was a bunch of us there, a team of auditors, four of us, and the minute he hit the key of the iron typewriter his hair stood straight up on his head, it's a wonder it didn't kill him! *"Oh My God!"* he said, *"the shock treatment all over again."* For a minute he thought he was back in the hospital again.

I mentioned that Nimshi was well known as an orator and debater. One time I went to a debate in which Nimshi was up against a very erudite luminary from academia and it looked like he would blow Nimshi out of the water. He went on for a long time making his points and Nimshi just sat there patiently waiting until he was done. Finally, his opponent concluded with a look of confidence saying, *"Now for the affirmative side, that is the sound argument I am making."* and sat down. Nimshi stood up, walked around the stage, pulled the lank hair out of his eyes and said, *"My worthy opponent says that was a sound argument in favour of the affirmative." "Here is another sound."* And he whistled. *"That sound is wind, and that was much of the argument that was made by my opponent."* He went on to win the debate.

Nimshi was a great nationalist, Newfoundland nationalist that is, as well as a great historian. In fact, after Confederation, he became the first archivist at the Newfoundland Archives. But at this time, which was before Confederation and during the war years, the British-led Commission of Government was running Newfoundland, as mentioned above. At any given time, there was only one Newfoundland member on the Commission, and many decisions were made that did not take into account the concerns and sensitivities of the Newfoundland people. The Commission had reinstituted a Nomenclature Board that had been brought into being by the Newfoundland government before it went bankrupt to find new names for the many ports, ponds, harbours and other landforms around the country that had wound up having the same name as one another because of the remoteness of much of the settlements in the early days and the fact that they would have had no idea that the names they were choosing were already in use elsewhere.

Nimshi Cole Crewe

Courtesy of Town of Elliston Website

Being an avid historian, Nimshi knew better than anyone the background of names from the days they were first used. He was really a staunch supporter of the unique place names of Newfoundland because he felt they expressed the feelings of the people so well. So while he might not have been disturbed by one or more of the many communities named "Island Cove" being renamed to distinguish these communities from one another, he took particular exception to what he viewed as British overlords and their effete sensitivities over some of the more colourful names that they wished to change to something more socially acceptable.

One day he came into the office and he was fit to be tied; you couldn't talk him down out of it. He said, *"Morry, you know what that damn Nomenclature Board has done?"* Now, I had rarely if ever heard Nimshi swear before so I knew he was really upset. I said, *"No, Sir."*

"Well," he said "they changed a number of old traditional names, some of them with good strong, sound names with longstanding connections to the areas where they are found to names that mean nothing. For instance, they called one place Cascades. What do you think of Cascades as a name for a place in Newfoundland, Morry?"

I thought for a while and, figuring there might have been a waterfall or rapids nearby I said, *"Well it's all according to how appropriate the new name is, Mr Crewe." "Well,"* he said *"it doesn't matter. I'll tell you, they changed 'Pissing Mare' to 'Cascades'. A fine virile name like that has such meaning and such strength, what does Cascades mean, they're all over the world?" "Well,"* I said, *"I guess it looks better on an envelope coming through the mail."* And he turned away in disgust and said, *"Morry, you missed the point entirely!"*

There was a local tavern in St. John's that I used to frequent that was called the *"Cottage Garden Tea Rooms"*. I never did figure out why they called it that, for there certainly had never been any intention of using it for that purpose. It was a tavern; not a low dive, but still a tavern. Perhaps it was a hold-over from Prohibition days when carefully disguised speakeasies were the only place you could get a drink. But I doubt it. Everyone knew what you went to this *"Tea Room"* for. Well, almost everyone.

One holiday we were sitting there and playing darts when this dainty little old lady came through the door, looked around for an empty table without any reprobates gathered around it, and then sat at one of the few unoccupied tables. Cooper, who was the bartender, and who was also the owner, a rough sort, but a good one, looked over at us with a quizzical look on his face and then proceeded over to the table where this distinguished lady was sitting to ask if he could help her, assuming, I suppose, that she was lost. She said, *"I'd like some tea please." "Tea!"*, he roared out, *"how the hell do you expect to get tea in here?"* The poor woman was taken aback by his rough demeanour and his language, as you might imagine. *"Well,"* she said, *"it says outside Cottage Garden Tea Room"*. He said, *"Ma'am, there's no tea served here. Anything we serve here comes out of a bottle and if you don't want that I can't help you."* The poor old dear gathered up her shopping bags and toddled out of there, everyone laughing irreverently as she went.

Another long weekend we were sitting around the *"Cottage"* as usual having a drink, getting set up for the weekend. We'd usually go around the bay somewhere or out to the Bella Vista late in the night. Anyway, a guy called Blair, who worked for the government as most of us did, came in. He had been living out of town around the bay for some years. And he was a notorious toper, a little short guy, but the man could drink like you wouldn't believe. Anyway, he had been down to the butcher's, Sandy Foster, and he had hung by a string on his arm the roast for his Sunday dinner. This was now Saturday morning. He had it hanging on his arm and the paper was beginning to show what was in there because it was not wrapped very well.

Anyway, we drank there for a couple of hours and I went off with Cooper to his place and we had a couple more in there. Then it was by now getting late so we got some girls to go out to the Bella Vista with us, but we had to stop into *"the Cottage"* for *"refreshment"* en route. There was Blair, still there, the roast still hanging on his arm, the Macintosh overcoat on the other, just as if he was going home; this was seven hours later. So, we went on to the Bella Vista and had a few in there and a dance and so on, when here comes a familiar figure, Blair. He crossed the dance floor looking for a table with the meat still hanging on his arm, with most of the paper now gone off of it. He sat down. We couldn't believe our eyes. Eventually, we went on or went home.

The next morning, there was a shebeen in Rabbittown we all knew where we could get a drink, a *"hair of the dog"* as they say to clear the morning after haze, and we all turned up there eventually on Sunday mornings.

[Editorial note: Rabbittown is the area of St. John's built for returning servicemen after WWI. It was no rougher than many other neighbourhoods, certainly not as rough as the Gower St. area at the time, but seemed to be a favourite place for informal "shebeens" or "speakeasies" in those days.]

Who walks in? Blair, the roast still on his arm! By this time, he was accompanied by a swarm of flies following him around. This was Sunday and a fairly warm day for Newfoundland, and he still had the meat on his arm twenty-four hours after we first saw him. The last I saw of him was that afternoon where we were playing a poker game and he still had it on his arm there, with no paper covering it at all. Now, by this time, it was beginning to smell. I do not know whatever happened or whether that meat ever made it home but I sincerely hope no one ever attempted to cook and eat it.

After Confederation, in 1949, I was responsible as a district auditor for a group of officers who had to visit all the outports, no matter how remote, to instruct the citizens and to collect, when possible, certain amounts due to the government for the employer's share of unemployment insurance benefits. To accomplish total coverage of all villages, it was necessary to hire small boats to go from village to village as the "Coastal Boats" operated by the government only called at larger ports.

*Tom Morry and Evelyn Wheeler at their Engagement, 1944
Morry Family Collection*

There were very few boats of the type required available for hire, as we had to have sleeping and dining accommodation aboard since commercial accommodation was not normally available ashore.

The boats usually had three bunks and could carry two passengers, and only a few of these boats had flush toilets. The owner of the boat was usually the Captain, engineer and cook, and the food which resulted from this combination would never appear in "Good Housekeeping" magazine or the "Michelin Guide". It was alright as long as they had a drink of rum to start out with but after the rum ran out it was pretty hard living.

On one trip, I was told the menu was bologna for 13 meals in a row and, when the passengers complained, they had salt mutton for the next ten meals before the voyage ended. The lack of refrigeration, sanitary facilities and proper care in the preparation of food often created havoc with the digestive system, and continuing diarrhea, or *"the runs"*, as it was known locally, was not uncommon.

One day, when we were visiting Twillingate Island, which at that time had no roads, we had to anchor the boat on the lee side of the island, which was far away from the village where the employers were located; there were usually only one or two in each place. One of the government men, a man named Kennedy, had the normal complaint. The boat had a flush toilet and, as he knew he would be finishing the trip that evening, he did not feel too bad.

Converting from Newfoundland to Canadian Civil Servant, March 28, 1949
Morry Family Collection

Before he left the boat, in the morning he spent considerable time on the toilet and he felt quite safe when he left to visit the employer, who lived about a mile away. The island, like many of its kind in the area, is completely barren, except for grass and a very low brush, and there was no shelter of any kind. About 3

PM, we were ready to leave, except that Kennedy hadn't yet returned, so we sounded the horn and stood on the dock to wait for him.

Soon after, we saw him coming toward us walking at a brisk pace, which he accelerated when he was about halfway between the employer's premises and the boat. It was a grey kind of day and he had on an overcoat and a hat. He passed the last small group of houses and increased his pace until he was running, briefcase in hand and coattails flying behind him. Suddenly he dropped the briefcase and started to remove his overcoat, which he dropped to the ground. Then his hat blew off and he didn't stop to pick it up, all the time quickening his speed. He was now running at full speed and, at first, we thought he must be hungry or needed a drink badly enough, but then we, who were observing the scene, could now see an expression of great anxiety on his face, for he was now within three or four hundred yards of the boat. Suddenly he slowed, then stopped and then, after several instants, started towards us again with a slow and somewhat ungainly walk until he reached the pier at which time, without any word of greeting or explanation he jumped into the cold water. The reason for the strange behaviour was of course obvious. He had felt *"the call"* soon after he left the employer's premises and gambled that he could make the boat in time. He lost!

On another trip, we encountered one old man in Harbour Deep in northern Newfoundland. When we went into his premises he said, *"Now who might you be, sor?"* He had the Excise people in, he had the Taxation people in, he had the Department of Labour and now he had this crowd, and we told him we're from the Unemployment Insurance and were here to ensure that you take care of the amounts you owe the government for the people who work for you. *"I got nobody working for me."* he said and I responded *"Oh yes you do, you sent in a form saying you have six people working for you. We've written you several letters and we got no reply."* He hauled a large box about three feet square from under the table he was sitting at and he said: *"Here, pick out your letters out of there and then we'll try to come to grips with them."*

Tom Morry, standing centre, and his UIC Audit Team, 1953
Morry Family Collection

And afterwards when I told him what he owed he was willing to pay. They weren't trying to avoid it, they just didn't understand these *"goddam forms"* and all the requirements. He said to me, he said *"We got one advantage in the outports, we don't have time for letters out here, sure you can write all the letters you like, if I don't want to answer them I just heave them in the box, that's all there's to it."* Then he said, *"I'm glad you came, now I got that many cleared up I can heave that many more in there."*

Newfoundlanders are very appreciative when anyone helps them, and usually find some way to demonstrate their gratitude. I do not know if civil servants in the provincial service had accepted token gifts in this fashion, but I do know that I had to discourage the practice many times on my own behalf and on behalf of my employees of the Government of Canada. In spite of this, some clients, particularly from rural areas, would insist and would arrive at our office with ducks, chickens, fish, vegetables and even moonshine on occasion to show their gratitude. I had explained the local custom to higher authorities and had been told that, short of creating animosity, all such gifts were to be refused and the local staff were to be told that they could lose their job if they accepted gifts.

In the early months and years of Confederation, there was a great influx of mainlanders sent down to the Newfoundland government offices to show the unlettered local staff how to do things, organizing the offices, etc. and the local staff were very wary of these strangers in the beginning. The mainlanders didn't quite know how to make out the Newfoundlanders. It took them quite a while to realise that they were a different breed of cat than they were used to dealing with. For instance, if you do something for a Newfoundlander, or even if you failed to do it but you tried, he'd likely come and give you a brace of rabbits or a brace of partridge or some codfish or something of that kind.

One day, a fisherman whom we had helped to get unemployment insurance even though he could not prove he had his *"stamps"*, arrived at the office with a gift for the officer who had helped him. He came to me first and insisted that he see the officer concerned, and told me he had some salt fish to give him. He needn't have told me what he had, I knew before he entered the door, for the unmistakable aroma preceded him. Salt fish normally has a very distinctive bouquet, but when it is not completely cured, and if it has received more rain than sun, the smell is even more pungent. This particular batch of fish was clearly in the latter category.

When the fisherman reached the office to which I had diverted him, two mainlanders were with the officer concerned, but this did not deter our caller, who marched into the office, laid the large odorous package on the desk and said: *"Me boy, I've brought you a little present"*. The officer placed the package back in the fisherman's hands but he threw it back on the desk and departed rapidly so as to avoid further argument.

When he had gone, the Newfoundland officer went into long explanations about how he didn't accept gifts and the mainlanders reassured him that they understood his position. I was able to reassure my employee that he would not lose his job because of that particular gift and that, moreover it would have been an insult and an injury to the man's pride if he had not accepted it. It was not considered a bribe in Newfoundland.

The cod was there all day, one of the few warm days we had that summer, and by the end of the day, the smell was something else for people not used to it. We distributed the cod amongst the office staff that would have some of it, as the two mainlanders were leaving the office, they doing their best to retain a solemn demeanour. As they passed me, they began to laugh and one said to the other "Poor Al, he's worried about that gift; I thought the caller had brought in something rotten to insult him."

It's often said that truth is stranger than fiction, and some of the things that happen in real life are more comical than those that are conceived and put together to get laughs. My sister, Phyl had a friend named John Ferguson.

[Editorial note: Real names are used. These are family members and they would not mind, and also enjoyed telling the story]

John was a Scotsman. I never saw him without a necktie and suit on, no matter where he was, whether he was at leisure or otherwise. And he and Phyl and my father used to go on occasional road trips around Newfoundland, during which they would picnic out regardless of the weather. In Newfoundland, picnics often consist of very strange food and drink, and this day they stopped near a little river and they cooked up some sausages, to which they added canned spaghetti and beans.

When all was ready, the food was put on paper plates and they sat down to eat. Now Phyl and my father, in typical Newfoundland fashion, found a rock to put the food down on and sat down beside it and ate. John, however, in the patrician manner to which he was accustomed, sat with his suit and necktie on and sat on the rock and tried to balance the plate on his knees. And in the course of cutting the sausage with a blunt knife, the plate went up in the air and came down bottom up on his clothes.

And here he was, sitting there with spaghetti and beans and sausages and whatever else was in the melange spread all over him. He just sat there; he didn't do anything. Phyl and my father, on the other hand, laughed so hard they very nearly fell into the little stream where they were and no attempt was made for about ten or fifteen minutes to do anything to help John, who was still sitting there, woebegone with the food all over him.

Eventually, they scraped him off and went on home. Every now and then they laughed so heartily that he told them he was going to refuse to drive them if they kept it up, and since neither of them could drive, they did have to attempt to control themselves. Anyway, the next day, the suit was in such a mess, Phyl called in the cleaners and handed the suit to the guy who came around to the door and he said, *"My God missus! That man must have been some sick"!*

I have referred earlier to the streak of irreverence which is usually a facet of the Newfoundlander's personality. The following story will demonstrate.

One of the strangest burials, or at least committal ceremonies, I ever attended happened in Ferryland a few years ago. A cousin of mine, Ern, had lived a rather dissolute life, working sporadically as a taxi-driver, but frequently going on binges which lasted for several days.

[Editorial note: The names have not been changed. The confusion between "Ern" and "Urn" would not work any other way. Besides, they are family!]

Like many alcoholics, this man, who was normally quiet and reserved, became difficult and frequently quarrelsome when he was on a binge. His family lived in a state of uneasiness, and his wife left him on a number of occasions when it became impossible to cope with him and when there was no money to keep the home going.

The children left home as soon as possible after they had finished high school and eventually the mother left to live with one of the children. There was very little contact between the father and any member of the family for several years and, eventually, he left the province to live in one of the large mainland cities. Here he lived on the government pension, welfare, sporadic earnings and handouts from his family and friends.

At last, the inevitable occurred and Ern died alone, but an acquaintance informed the family of his death. After a discussion of what was to be done, one of the children who lived in Boston and who was more affluent than the others, arranged for cremation and the ashes were sent to Newfoundland in the mail, as she felt he would want his ashes to be scattered at home in Ferryland, which he loved, although he wasn't born there, rather than on the mainland.

This daughter, who visited the province each year in the summer, wired my sister-in-law in Newfoundland saying "Urn arriving next week; please take care of him until I arrive in about three weeks." Pat, who received the wire, assumed that someone had misspelled Ern as Urn and did not know what to do. She knew

Ernie's habits and she wondered how she was going to cope with his drinking for two or three weeks, and she waited with apprehension for his arrival.

One day, when the mail arrived, she received a small metal box, without explanation and, as the inside wrapper was marked *"Hold for Mrs. Thomson"*, she threw it up on one of the shelves in the cupboard to await Ruth's arrival.

Ruth duly arrived, but Pat forgot about the package until one night during a party, when all present had had many drinks. When the box was produced, Ruth said: "Oh, this is the Urn, we must have a committal service".

The night was dark and windy, but after a few more drinks, it was decided that it was time to consign Ern's ashes to the waters of Ferryland Harbour, as he would have wanted, and three or four of the group went to the beach and out on the Morry wharf to dispose of the remains. We brought with us some glasses and a bottle of rum and, after pouring a drink, we prepared to scatter the ashes on the sea. We found that the box could not be opened so one of the group took a large stone and, after some difficulty, made a hole in the box. Then all raised their glasses and drank to Ern while the ashes were thrown into the sea. There was still a breeze blowing towards the land and much of the ashes were blown back on the "Committal Party". Whether anyone knew it at the time or not is difficult to say, but when we arrived back in the house the drinking glasses still contained a residue of Ernie, but this did not seem to affect anyone. The toast was proposed after which the incident was forgotten. Ernie must have been quite happy with the service, if he was looking on from the other world, considering his fondness for rum, but in terms of respect, the burial left something to be desired and some of those who had been present probably wished that they had not been.

Chapter 7: Becoming a "CFA"

Editorial Notes:

I don't suppose there is anyone, even a Yank or a Mainlander, who doesn't know what a CFA is anymore. Not since the Broadway musical about Newfoundland hospitality after 9-11, anyway. But to be sure, it stands for "Come From Away". As the 9-11 incident amply demonstrated, CFAs are welcome in Newfoundland, even if Newfoundlanders cannot understand why they would live anywhere else. But, as in Dad's case, sometimes that less fortunate status is forced upon you by circumstances beyond your control.

My father concluded his memoirs with three short anecdotes that related to his jobs after moving to the mainland in 1953. The reason for this move was simple; he had joined the federal Public Service (Unemployment Insurance Commission - UIC) after Confederation (the topic of several of the anecdotes above) and, in a matter of three or four years, had risen to the top of the ranks in that organization in Newfoundland. Any future career progression would necessitate a move to Ottawa.

The decision to make this move would not have been taken lightly. It was a devastating event for grandparents on both sides of the family. In addition, not only would they be leaving their friends and family, but for my mother, she would be leaving the only place she had ever lived – a place that she loved and regretted leaving till the day that she died. But, like so many Newfoundlanders before him, Dad realised that he could not achieve his full potential at home, and so, very reluctantly, they agreed that the move was necessary, and he decided to accept the transfer.

These three little anecdotes, two pertaining to the time just after the move to Ottawa, when he was still working for what was then called the UIC, and the other some years later when he had risen in the ranks through promotions and transfers to become the Assistant Deputy Minister (Civilian Personnel) at the Department of National Defence, don't capture even slightly the momentous events in his life after leaving Newfoundland. But I suspect that when he wrote his memoirs, his real intention was to focus on life in Newfoundland, and anything that took place elsewhere, such as in the US or in mainland Canada, was only secondary to his intent.

When I came to Ottawa, the first building where I worked was over by Preston and Carling. It was an old wooden building called Number 8 because it was one of the so-called "Temporary Buildings" built during the war to accommodate activities related to the war effort but that was still going strong then and even many years later in the '60s when I left there, and it was torn down in the '80s and was replaced with a parking lot for tourists visiting Dow's Lake and the Rideau Canal, nearby.

Demolition of temporary buildings at Dow's Lake, April 17, 1980
Photograph from the Ottawa Citizen

I found to my surprise that there were a bunch of rare characters working there, just as there had been at many of my workplaces in Newfoundland. A lot of them had served in the war and they were devil-may-care types, having survived those devastating and life-altering events. You had to like them but they were pretty hard to manage, as I used to supervise them.

When I worked in *"Standards and Methods"* I had a couple of fellas working for me, one named Mack and another fella that always went by his last name, Farrell. They were low-level clerks, sometimes called *"gophers"* because they would be sent to the archives to *"go for"* the files that were being worked on in the office that day. They had a co-worker, by the name of Harvey, who was most likely suffering from what we now know as Post Traumatic Stress Disorder (PTSD) and the poor man seemed to have the whole world on his back. He demonstrated all kinds of odd behaviours that made him a target for the *"normal"* staff members like Mack and Farrell.

For example, at lunchtime, he used to put his lunch in a drawer in the desk and reach in and take a bite out of his sandwich like a rat, and then hide it in the drawer again. He had built for himself out of cardboard and sticky tape a frame or sort of privacy shield that he put on his desk and would crouch down behind so that no one would see him and he could see no one while he was eating his lunch. The other guys used to throw things at him over the barrier just to get his goat, but he still persisted in eating his lunch in that manner.

Harvey worked harder than any of the others in the office, but he was always complaining of the antics (today we would say harassment) of Mack and Farrell and one day he came to me and said that I should do something, so I went to the two of them and said, *"For crying out loud, guys, leave him alone; don't ride him so much, he's on the verge."* But they kept it up. For instance, they used to sing a song that went *"Molly was a lady until she fell"*, and Harvey's wife was named Molly.

In those days, not only did you have to sign in and sign out when you came to work and left, but they used to ring bells to tell you when you were permitted to leave for lunch and at the end of the day. At 5 o'clock, needless to say, Harvey was right on the mark ready to leave the torment behind, and he used to grab his coat off the hook and be out the door before the bell had stopped ringing, pretty impressive for a man of forty or fifty years of age, and he would run down the street and be number one on the bus home. So, the boys were watching him do this for some time, and still stinging from the reprimand that I gave them over their treatment of Harvey. They thought to themselves, *"Well, we'll get that sonofabitch."* So, one of them brought in a six-inch nail and they nailed Harvey's overcoat onto the wooden wall. That evening the five o'clock bell rang and Harvey made his usual dash to get out of the office, grabbed hold of his coat, which he was used to just grabbing on the way and putting on once he got outside, and he swung out of it because it was nailed firmly to the wall. All hell broke loose and Harvey didn't get out in time for the bus.

And he came down to me and what he didn't call everybody concerned, including me! Naturally, I had to take action, and I had to suspend the two perpetrators, but they were happy enough to take the punishment and were still laughing about the incident years later. I bumped into Mack when he was retired and was then working as a Commissionaire out to the airport and the first thing he said to me was, *"Do you remember Harvey?" "Indeed, I do,"* I replied.

Another character at Building 8 was a man named Les, also a war veteran. He had been fairly old during the war because he retired long before these other guys. He was a great man for the bottle. The job he had was to store all the books in the "catacombs" under the building. Everybody receiving unemployment insurance had a book in which payments were recorded. He loved this job because it gave him the opportunity to be on his own, and to be able to have a drink or two during the day. I've seen him come up out of there in the evening at the end of the day and normally he would be very courteous and courtly saying goodbye to everyone as they departed for the day but, more than once he was so high he could barely stand up, and he would lean against the door frame and at times he could barely move his lips to speak. Fortunately, in those post-war years, very few people could afford a car and he travelled home by bus like everyone else. Other than this foible, which may have been a carryover from his war experiences, he enjoyed life to the fullest and in fact, he could normally walk straighter when he was drunk than most people can when they are sober. He was an endearing character, but one that today would probably lose his job out of hand. Times change. Sometimes not for the better.

When I was with National Defence, we once brought in a bunch of junior personnel officers who were stationed in faraway military bases, many of them in Germany, and hence who never got a chance to be exposed to much training of any kind at their workplaces. They were good employees because they had to operate more or less independently without easy recourse to the advice and resources available to those who worked at headquarters in Ottawa. They had to cover off every aspect of personnel management and many of them had little training to start out with.

Business card, T. G. Morry
Assistant Deputy Minister (Manpower), National Defence
Morry Family Collection

So, we booked the group into the Lord Elgin Hotel, because the government rates were pretty good there in those days, in fact, that is where my family was placed for a week or ten days when we first came to Ottawa before I had a chance to find an apartment. As I say, they were from remote areas and usually had been recruited in those areas and didn't have any experience staying in hotels of this kind.

About the second day, I was going around getting to know them all and I stopped to talk to one and said, *"Well, Robert, how are you making out?"* and he said *"Great. Great hotel."* I think it was the first hotel he had ever stayed in. He said, *"I always thought that the people in Ottawa, were stuck up and unfriendly but I've never met such friendly people in my life."*

It transpired that what had happened was that, the night before, he had gone down to the bar in the lobby of the Elgin after dinner and a few minutes after entering the bar a bunch of local guys came up and spoke to him and bought him a couple of drinks. He said, *"If it hadn't been for the fact that we had meetings today I would have gone on with them when they moved on to another bar, but I invited them to come to my room tonight for a party."* I said, *"Will they bringing some girls with them?"* and he said, *"Now that you mention it, I didn't see any girls there."* What he did not know, was that the bar at the Lord Elgin was the only well-known gay bar in Ottawa in those days. The gay guys he met were only too happy to make his acquaintance as a newcomer to their fold! I had to explain to him the situation and I'm sure that was the end of the plans for the party in his room that evening.

But another bunch was brought in for training in Québec City and were put up in what was rather a posh hotel there, surprisingly, considering the limitations on government accommodation standards. It was the first place I ever saw bars in the rooms. You didn't put in any money; you just took what you wanted and they tallied it up and charged you when you were leaving. Anyway, after dinner, we had a couple of drinks and then I went to my room.

But one of the people there on training stayed on. He had a wonderful singing voice and the people in the bar kept him in drinks until the bar closed, and then they went back to his room to keep the thing going. He later told me, *"Too bad you didn't stay, we had a great time back at my room."* I said, *"I suppose you did, but where did you get the liquor at that time of night."* He said, *"Don't you know you have a free bar in your room? We all had a great time. We drank everything in the cabinet."* I said to him, *"My friend, let me tip you off. Before you leave this evening, go up to the front desk and ask what your bill will be so you can get out enough money from the bank to pay the damages."* He said, *"What do you mean damages?"* And I told him, and he turned white as a sheet and ran off to the front desk. A few minutes later he caught up with me in the training room and said, *"$163!"* and I said, *"Now you know why that bar is there. For people to have an occasional drink when it's too late to buy a bottle but not to have a party. There are cheaper ways to have a party."* This training session taught him a valuable, but expensive, lesson!

Cartoon Presented to Tom Morry on leaving National Defence

Epilogue/Conclusion

"Now to conclude and finish, the truth to you I'll tell...."

For those of you not familiar with Newfoundland folk songs, that is the apt first line of the last verse of "The Star of Logy Bay".

My father left Newfoundland when he was 34 years old. He lived until he was in his 89th year, worked until the day that he died, and, from the day he could first afford it, he and Mom spent their summer vacations "at home" in Newfoundland -- forty years or more enriching Air Canada and Rent-A-Wreck! In that respect, he was a typical expatriate Newfoundlander, but he was also typical of that odd breed of cat in that he never became an Ontarian, though he spent more of his life there than in Newfoundland. On the other hand, he was a fiercely proud Canadian and staunch supporter of Confederation. Which, of course, was the cause of no end of heated battles with his brother Bill and many other Newfoundlanders whose *"misguided"* opinion was that Newfoundland would have fared better on her own.

Also like most expatriate Newfoundlanders who left home to make a decent living for themselves and their family, he did much more than just make a decent living; he excelled at what he did, rising from his humble beginnings with no more than a high school education to achieve the top echelons of the Canadian Public Service (not that that would have won him many kudos at home!).

Before he died, he penned and recorded the anecdotes that comprise this volume, not because he expected to make money off of his efforts, since he had no intention of publishing his memoirs in his lifetime. Nor less still to make fun of the people he encountered during his life, though some reading these stories could be excused for thinking that. He recorded these stories out of a sense of pride that he had had the privilege of knowing such a diverse, endearing, and yes, bizarre and strange, group of Newfoundlanders, but also in the realization that he was not alone in this and that anyone who lived their lives in Newfoundland would recognise characters in this book as being virtually identical to people that they had grown up with.

Newfoundland, possibly because of its isolation from the rest of the world, or possibly because of its harsh environment and the even harsher economic conditions that long prevailed there, has been producing characters like these from the days of its earliest settlement. I hope that in retelling these stories here on Dad's behalf, I have done justice to his memory and brought a smile or two of recognition to those Newfoundlanders who read the stories and that no one takes too much offence from them.

To quote a line from another of Dad's favourite old Newfoundland folk songs, actually, a folk song brought over to Ferryland from Devon by the Morry immigrant ancestor Matthew Morry in the late 1700s – "Bachelor's Hall": *"if there's anyone here who takes any offence, he (she) can go to the Devil and seek recompense!"*

Acknowledgments

First and last thanks go to Dad, for having had the foresight to record his memories on paper and sound recording. Although all these anecdotes had been heard by everyone in the family numerous times, none of us ever thought to write them down, because Dad was invincible and would never die, or so we thought. In one sense at least, that is true, because he will now live on through these stories, which will be passed on to future generations.

Also, a special thanks to Mom for having put up with this weird character for a lifetime, allowing him the freedom to be himself and regale all and sundry with his stories and songs from Newfoundland. Dad had an eye for beauty, especially in the female of the species, and a fondness for a good drink and good cigars and it took a very special kind of woman to live with the likes of him.

Several poor souls volunteered (actually were Shanghaied) to review the manuscript of this book again and again until I finally got it more or less right. These included my friend and partner in genealogical research, Kevin Reddigan. Cyril and Enid O'Brien verified that I would not (necessarily) be lynched for putting this out there the next time that I am in Ferryland. Also, my younger brother Glen, who, though he suffers from a major failing of NOT being a Newfoundlander, has two degrees in Psychology and hence was able to set me straight on quite a number of scores. I hold these people entirely blameless for what you see before you.

Finally, I would like to thank you, the reader. My father was never so happy as he was when he had an audience to regale with his stories. You are giving him an extended stay on this earth and, in that sense, his one-man show has been *"held over"*.

Appendix

Awards and Honours

I am inclined to think that Dad's rapid rise in public service in the field of personnel management is a testament to his upbringing in Newfoundland. Newfoundlanders are by nature good-spirited individuals inclined to give those around them the benefit of the doubt. This, as it turns out, is an essential element of good personnel management. The fact that Dad could combine this with his own laconic nature, his joie de vivre and his absolute joy in being with others and having a *"time"*, meant that he was destined from the beginning to go far in his chosen field.

The results speak for themselves. Here are a small number of the testaments, honours and awards recognising the high esteem in which he was held by his peers and the governments that he served for 44 years.

Canadian Public Personnel Management Association Biography of Thomas Graham Morry, 1978 On the Occasion of Awarding Him Honorary Life Membership

Mr. Morry was born in Ferryland, Newfoundland and was educated in Newfoundland the U.S.A. He joined the Public Service of Canada in 1949 as District Auditor for the Unemployment Commission following service with the Government of Newfoundland in a number of accounting and financial capacities.

In 1953, he was appointed to a position with the U.I.C. in Ottawa and two years later became Director of Enforcement.

He was appointed Director of Personnel of the U. I. C. in 1958 and in 1960, Director of combined Personnel, Administration and Finance Branches. In January 1965, he was seconded to the Public Service Commission to implement the proposals of the Glassco Commission regarding Personnel Administration.

In November 1966, he was appointed Director of the Administration Staffing Programs for the Public Service and in 1967, he was named Assistant Deputy Minister, Personnel, Department of National Defence of Canada.

In 1975, Mr. Morry went on language training and following this, he was appointed Director-General of the Anti-Discrimination Branch of the P.S.C. effective January 1976. He was appointed to his present position, Executive Director, Appeals and Investigations Branch, effective January 1, 1978.

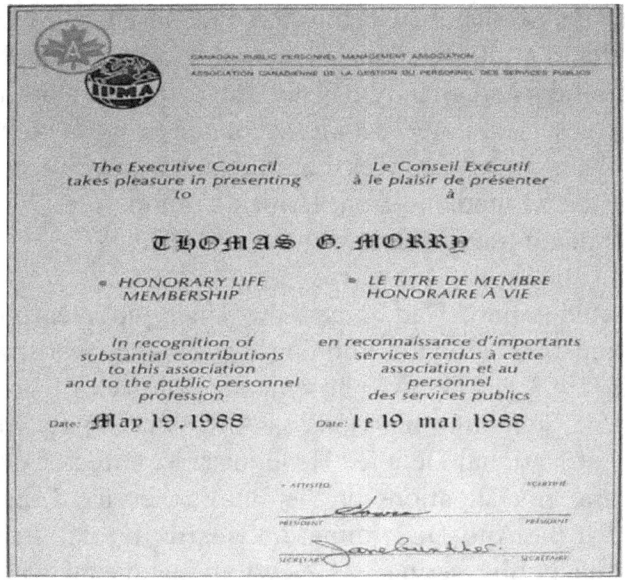

International Personnel Management Association Names Award in Honour of Thomas Graham Morry

(Text of a speech given by his son, Howard Glendon Morry, at the presentation of the T. G. Morry for Excellence in Human Resources award in June 2008)

Dad died suddenly, taken peacefully in his sleep on Thursday, May 1st, 2008 in his 89th year. He was born in 1919 in the small fishing community of Ferryland, Newfoundland. He grew up in a large family where dependence on the sea for their survival made life difficult, but where storytelling and music filled the household and made life joyous and memorable.

Dad's career was a real "rags to riches" story. After finishing school in Newfoundland, he moved to the USA to work and pursue further studies in Boston and Pittsburgh. He returned to Newfoundland at the start of the Second World War and because his two brothers had already enlisted, he ended up working in the war services sector. Later, he was seconded to work with English and Canadian representatives completing arrangements for the transfer of Newfoundland from British Commission Government rule to Canadian provincehood.

After Confederation, Dad joined the Unemployment Insurance Commission in St. John's, winning a promotion and transfer to Ottawa in 1953. In Ottawa, he enjoyed a series of progressive appointments including positions as Assistant Deputy Minister – Personnel at National Defence Headquarters, Director General of Appeals and Investigations at the Public Service Commission, and Head of the Anti-Discrimination Board. In total, he spent 44 years in the public service of Newfoundland and Canada and loved every minute of it.

He used to say he couldn't wait to get out of bed in the morning – his work excited him that much. His devotion to the Public Service must have rubbed off on his children, because they all followed in his footsteps – his daughter Lanny with the CRTC and CBC, Tom junior with Agriculture, the PSC and Treasury Board, Chris with Fisheries and Oceans, and Glen with Canada Post, the PSC and now the RCMP.

Dad served as President of the Public Personnel Management Association (in the US and Canada) and as a result, he was made an honorary life member of both IPMA-Canada and IPMA-HR. There are only two such recipients and this was quite an honour for him.

He had a passion for Human Resources issues and kept in touch with his colleagues in the IPMA and the unions. Dad was always a strong supporter of a professional HR Community in the National Capital Region and around the country. All who knew him respected him for his breadth and depth of knowledge. Unhappy with retirement, Dad continued working as a consultant, maintaining his focus on anti-discrimination and the rights of employees to dignity and a fair and equitable workplace. In fact, he continued to work right up to the day before he died.

I know Dad was thrilled that IPMA Canada created this award in his honour, though I am sure he'd rather be here today to bestow the award himself, rather than have it given posthumously!

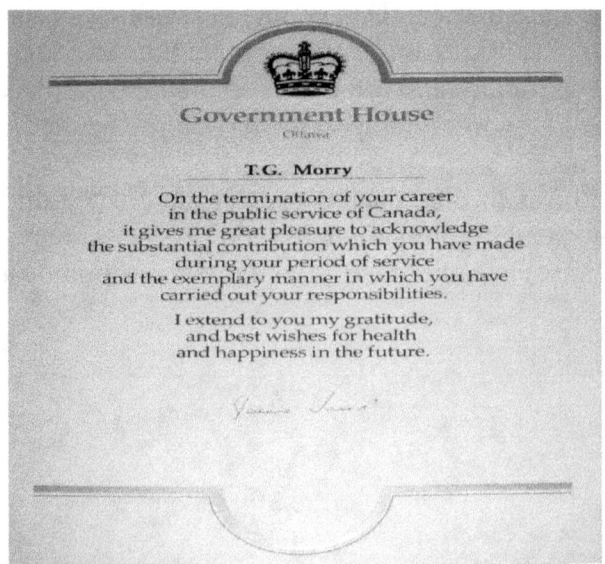

Thomas G. Morry

*On the occasion of your retirement
from the Public Service,
I wish to thank you on behalf
of the Government and people of Canada
for 44 years of loyal service
and to extend to you
our best wishes.*

84.12.04

Prime Minister

THE PREMIER

THE GOVERNMENT OF THE PROVINCE
OF NEWFOUNDLAND AND LABRADOR

November 26, 1984.

Mr. T.G. (Tom) Morry,
c/o Public Service Commission of Canada,
Ottawa, Canada.

Dear Sir:

    On the occasion of your retirement from the Public Service Commission of Canada, following some forty-four (44) years of distinguished service, permit me to extend on behalf of the Government and people of your native Province, sincere congratulations on the attainment of this significant achievement and to express best wishes for good health and happiness in the years ahead.

    As the unofficial Ambassador of goodwill from Newfoundland and Labrador in Ottawa, your accomplishments in promoting the friendly Province have been symbolic of your loyalty and personal commitment to the service of your fellow citizens at home and abroad. In the traditional salutation of a fellow Newfoundlander - "Long May Your Big Jib Draw".

Yours sincerely,

A. BRIAN PECKFORD, P.C., M.H.A.,
PREMIER.

And a few more humorous *"awards"* (?)…

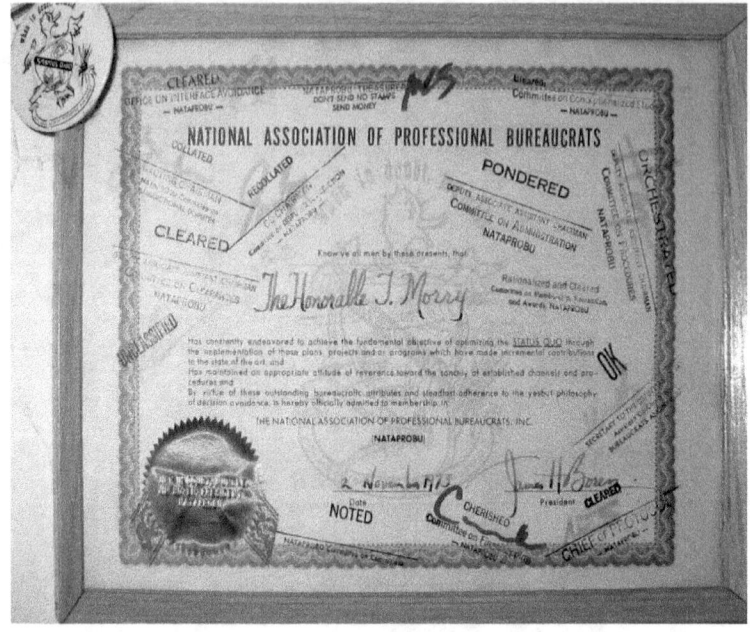

TOM MORRY

Believes

- Newfie jokes must be kept simple for mainlanders to understand them
- Accepting Canada into Confederation was a smart move by Newfoundland
- Confederation requires firm Newfoundland hands at the helm
- Yellow bow ties and purple trousers are a reasonable compromise between fishermen's oilskins and the grey flannel suits of mandarin-land
- Attractive women look better than unattractive ones
- He has got DND functioning smoothly and it is time to take all his languages and move on

The Facts

- Mainlanders do not even understand simple Newfie jokes
- Canadian dialects have ruined the purity of Newfoundland speech
- We are in danger of becoming a trilingual country with so many Newfoundlanders at the helm
- Yellow bow ties and purple trousers are an offence to the unimaginative
- Unattractive women can get on with their jobs
- Smoothness isn't everything — DND will miss the Heart and Character of

THE BEAU BRUMMEL OF THE EX SET

[1] T. G. Morry, bottom right, playing chess.

About the Editor

Christopher (Chris, CJ) Morry, was the second son of Tom and Evelyn Morry, born in St. John's on May 25, 1949. Having been born just after Canada joined Newfoundland, he has suffered from a lifelong inferiority complex, because he was not born a *"true"* Newfoundlander. He has tried to console himself that at least he was conceived when Newfoundland was a Dominion!

After completing a B.A. and an M.Sc. in the arcane field of Limnology (the science of freshwater ecosystems), and stints in Australia and New Zealand, he accepted an offer to come work for the Department of Fisheries and Oceans in his home town. In the following years, he worked on projects related to human impacts on both marine and freshwater environments across Newfoundland, in Labrador and in the offshore, in the early days of oil and gas exploration.

The rest of his career was spent essentially touring the country from coast, to coast to coast, as we say nowadays, offering advice in his chosen field, finishing off after a full career in the Public Service, with a five-year stint as a consultant, earning twice what he made in his best year working for government. Such is life!

Though he has authored numerous scientific and technical publications, the writing bug didn't really strike until his retirement years. His first book, *When the Great Red Dawn is Shining*, published by Breakwater Books in 2014, concerned his grandfather's experiences in WWI as a private in the Royal Newfoundland Regiment, in Gallipoli and on the Western Front. His second book, *The Last of the West Country Merchants*, self-published in 2019, is a synthesis of his 25 years of family history research, focussing on the family's immigrant ancestor, Matthew Morry. The present book is the last in the *"Morry Trilogy"*.

www.ingramcontent.com/pod-product-compliance
Lightning Source LLC
Chambersburg PA
CBHW070906080526
44589CB00013B/1196